A 52 WEEK STUDY

KNOWING
HIM

Transform your life by discovering the heart,
mind and will of the Father and the Son

STEVEN K SCOTT & DR. MICHAEL SMALLEY

Published by Knowing Him
© 2016 Steven K. Scott
Adapted from the book, *Jesus By Your Side,* by Steven K. Scott

Knowing Him
26205 Oak Ridge Drive, Suite 119
The Woodlands TX 77380

ISBN

To order additional copies of this resource, visit www.knowinghim.com

Printed in the United States of America

Other Resources From Knowing Him

Following Christ DVD and Workbook
Following Christ Online Course
The Greatest Words Ever Spoken
Jesus Speaks (365 Day Devotional)

You can purchase any of these resources online at www.knowinghim.com.

Table of Contents

Knowing Him Small Group Meetings

The heart of Knowing Him is to provide believers with an accelerated means of coming to know Jesus Christ more intimately, follow Him more fully, and lead others into that same kind of intimate relationship with Christ. Jesus said, "My sheep hear My voice, I know them and they follow Me. (John 10:27)

Our hope is you experience Jesus in a new way through the power of a small group. Meetings focused exclusively on the life and teachings of Jesus will give you a new passion to serve and follow Him like never before. Jesus said, "And this is eternal life, that they might know You, the only true God, and Jesus Christ whom you have sent." (John 17:3). By coming to know Christ more intimately, you also come to know the Father more intimately. In the Knowing Him small group format, you can take the commands and teachings of Christ, from the pages of your Bible, into the daily application and transformation of your life.

Knowing Him group meetings are not Bible studies, and do not require leaders who are skilled Bible teachers. They have a simple format in which the group facilitates the study time by simply asking six questions. No skills are necessary to attend or host a Knowing Him small group meeting. The only requirement is that the people attending desire to get to know the Lord Jesus Christ more intimately. Knowing Him groups are designed to multiply. Anyone who attends a Knowing Him small group, will be fully equipped to branch off and host a Knowing Him group of their own within six months of attending a Knowing Him group.

The meeting model

A Knowing Him group may consist of any small group, ranging from two people to twenty. It can be a men's or women's group, a mixed group, adults or youth. It can meet once a week, once every two weeks or even once a month. (Once a week or once every two weeks is what we would suggest)

Beginning

Like most small group meetings, the Knowing Him meeting begins with fellowship, sharing and prayer. You can use this time to meet and share personal application of the teaching of Christ that was studied at the previous week's meeting. It is an opportunity to keep each other accountable to the action steps talked about from the previous week's study.

Study Time

You will notice how each week has a "Special Insight". This can be read on your own or as a group. It just depends on what your group prefers. The study time begins with the group reading the selected statement of Christ in its context. This means you will want to read the verses before or after the statement included on the right side of the workbook.

Then, each individual writes in their own words, what they believe Jesus is saying. The area for this is provided in the left column under the quoted command from Christ. This is an important step of the study because it helps you fully integrate the command of Christ. It helps you think it through more thoroughly.

At this point you want to begin a discussion as a group by answering the six questions presented in the "S.P.E.C.K.S." format. As the group gives its answers to these questions, individuals can write down any answers that are helpful to their understanding of Christ's statement that is being studied.

S.P.E.C.K.S QUESTIONS

The questions that will be discussed in each meeting about the scripture being studied are:

S.   Are there any sins that we should try to avoid?
P.   Are there any implied or stated promises of Christ?
E.   Is there an "example" to follow in the context that surrounds this statement of Christ?
C.   Are there any implied or stated commands of Christ?
K.   What knowledge have I gained that I should begin to apply to my life?
S.   What's the "spirit" of this statement?

Here's an example of what this might look like for you:

Statement of Christ: "Do you not say there are yet four months and then comes the harvest?" I tell you, 'Look up, behold the fields are ready to harvest.'" John 4:35

In Your Own Words

Jesus is telling me to open my eyes and be attentive to what is right in front of me in the moment that I am in. He's telling me to not wait for opportunities to minister to others, but to minister to the people that are right in front of me at any moment that they come into my path. He's telling me to live in the moment and not the future or the past. He's telling me to harvest or take advantage of the opportunities that are right in front of me.

What "S.P.E.C.K.S." Do We See?

S. Are there any sins to avoid?
Yes. Don't live in the future or the past. Don't procrastinate ministry. Don't be distracted by concerns for the future or problems of the past. To not be attentive to the moment and ignore the opportunity that's right in front of me, is to disobey Jesus' teaching to live in the moment and make the most of it.

P. Are there any promises, implied or stated.
Yes. Jesus implies the promises that if I am attentive to living in the moment, I will reap a harvest, and bear fruit that will change lives and glorify God.

E. Is there an example to follow?
Yes. Jesus' encounter with the woman at the well. If Jesus had been living in the future or the past, even five minutes in the future or five minutes in the past, He would have missed the opportunity to minister to the woman. She would have not become a follower of Christ. She would not have witnessed to the people in her village. They would have not come out to see Jesus. And they would have not been redeemed or discipled in the two days that followed. Many lives were saved and transformed during the next 48 hours because Jesus lived in the moment, instead of the past or future.

C. Are there any Commands of Christ, stated or implied?
Yes. He states the command to look up and become focused on the opportunity that is right in front of me in the moment I'm in. He implies the command that I am to reap the harvest by taking the opportunity to minister in that moment. He implies the command that I am not to procrastinate ministry or wait for opportunities in the future. He implies the command that I am not to live in the future or the past but I am to focus entirely on the moment I am in and on the people that share that moment with me.

K. Is there knowledge I can take away and apply to the rest of my life?

If I want to experience all that God has for me, I must begin to live in the moment. God doesn't dwell in the future or the past, but only in the present moment. If I want to experience Him in my daily life, I must live in the moment. All fear and worry comes when I am focusing on the future, and all regret, disappointment, anger and bitterness comes when I'm focusing on the past. But God and all that He is and has, and all miracles happen in the moment.

S. What is the Spirit of this passage?

I can glorify God and serve others only when I'm in the moment. God is not going to punish me when I dwell in the future or past, but I will miss out on the incredible love He expresses in the moment. He loves me so much, I want to enjoy Him more by living in His moment with Him.

This format (for the most part) was originated by David Watson and published in his book, *Contagious Disciple Making*.

Now the group proceeds to the "I Will," portion of the study.

This is where each individual writes out specifically how they will apply what they've learned from Christ's statement in the coming week. For example, how they will apply it to their day, situations they face at work, or their relationships. This exercise enables each member of the group to take a teaching of Christ, break it down to their own understanding, and then let it impact their behavior and decisions in the week ahead. This is what Jesus meant when He said, "If you abide in My word, you'll be My disciples indeed, and you will know the truth, and the truth will make you free." (John 8:31-32)

1 Believe in God, Believe in Christ

Special Insight

Jesus commands His followers to have faith in God and to Believe (trust) in God and in Christ. These are truly the foundational commands upon which our relationship with the Father and Son will stand. They are also the necessary foundation upon which all of the other commands and promises of Christ will securely rest.

Jesus Concept of Belief and Faith is Very Different Than Ours!

In our modern culture, when we use words like believe, belief or faith, we are really referring to an opinion that we accept or embrace. For example we might say, "I believe it's going to rain tomorrow." That's not a belief, it's an opinion. We might say, "I believe I'm going to get a raise at work." Once again, that is merely an opinion or a wish. Sadly, for most people, their beliefs about Jesus and God the Father are little more than opinions that they accept be true. When someone says, "I believe that God exists and that Jesus is His Son," it is usually nothing more than an opinion they accept in their mind. However, if that statement is a true belief, then their entire life, everything they do, their words, attitudes and actions will flow out of that belief and reflect it. When Jesus used words like believe, trust, or faith, He was not talking about an opinion.

The Greek word *pisteo,* is the root word for faith, belief and trust. It literally means: to rely entirely upon or act upon. If I were sitting next to you and told you that I just got a call from a world-renowned geo-physicist who told me we were minutes away from a massive earthquake, you would react one of two ways. If you believed me, you would instantly warn your family and then run to the nearest secure place to hide. If you said you believed me, but continued to sit in your easy chair and watch TV, then regardless of what you said, your actions say you don't really believe me, but instead reflect your true belief that an earthquake wasn't about to strike. The truth is, our attitudes and actions always express our true beliefs!

Friend, if you are saying, "I want this kind of faith, but I don't know how to get it," I've got great news! Jesus has revealed exactly how you can grow your faith. He promises even the newest believers, "If you abide in my word, you are truly my disciples, and you will know the truth, and the truth will set you free." (John 8:31-32 ESV). That's all you have to do. It's that simple. Begin to abide in the words of Jesus, and over time, your seeds of faith with grow into a forest of mighty oaks.

Additional References for Study: Jesus Speaks, *May 10;* Greatest Words,
Belief and Faith in Christ (445-51)

Statement of Christ

"Have faith in God." Mark 11:22
"Believe in God, believe also in Me." John 14:1 (NASB)

In my own words	SPECKS	I will
	Sin	
	Promise (implied or stated)	
	Example	
	Command (implied or stated)	
	Knowledge	
	Spirit	

2 Don't Let Your Heart be Troubled

Special Insight

This command is so important to our daily life and fellowship with God, that Jesus gave it twice during His last supper with His Disciples.   In addition to His command, this statement gives three revelations about the "heart." It's important to realize that when Jesus talks about the heart, he's not talking about the beating organ beneath our chest. He's talking about the very core of our nature, the very essence of who we are. Jesus taught that all of our natural behavior flows out of the heart. Solomon taught the same, and was inspired by the Holy Spirit to write, "Above all else, guard your heart, for everything you do flows from it." (Proverbs 4:35 NIV).

Three Revelations About Our Heart

First, we can take control of our hearts. Instead of our heart ruling us, we can rule our heart. Second, when our hearts are troubled, filled with worry, stress or fear, there is a way that we can take charge of our heart and replace the worry, stress or fear with a supernatural peace that Jesus wants to give us. Third, there is only one way to take control of our heart, and that is to obey His command to Believe in Him and the Father. As we have seen earlier, the way we gain that kind of belief or trust in any given moment or situation is by hearing Jesus' words and doing them.

So in John 14: 1, Jesus commands us to do both—(1) take control of our heart and don't let it be troubled, and (2) Believe or trust in Him and the Father. When we will set our focus expressing our Belief in Him by abiding in His words and acting upon them, obey His command to take control of our heart and fill it with Belief in Him and the Father. As we actively trust Jesus and the Father, we will receive the supernatural, incomprehensible peace that Christ wants to flow into our hearts.

At any given moment, we can believe in His words, act upon them and receive His peace. But these are moment-by-moment choices that we make every day. As we saw with Peter's walking on water, you can be trusting Jesus and His words at one moment, and replace that trust with unbelief in the next. That's why controlling your heart, believing in Him and acting on His words are not once in a lifetime choices, but moment-by-moment choices.

> Additional References for Study: Jesus Speaks, January 3; Greatest Words, Anxiety,
> *Worry and Fear (190-93)*

Statement of Christ

"Do not let your hearts be troubled. You believe in God; believe also in me." John 14:1
"Do not let your hearts be troubled and do not be afraid." John 14:27

In my own words	SPECKS	I will
	Sin	
	Promise (implied or stated)	
	Example	
	Command (implied or stated)	
	Knowledge	
	Spirit	

3 Abide in His Word, Become His Disciple

Special Insight

Have you ever wondered what you should say to someone when they are first born again—when they are a brand new believer? Or, if you were asked by any believer, new or old, "What is the *key* to following Christ," or, "What can I do to *grow* my faith and have the strongest relationship possible with God?" Jesus answers these questions in John 8:31-32. He was speaking to people who had just become "believers" in Him. In verse 30, John tells us, "As He spoke these words, many believed in Him." Jesus' very first statement to these new believers was an extraordinary *conditional* promise—a promise that He would fulfill in their lives *if* they would meet His one condition. And because He made this promise to brand new believers, it is a universal principal that is available to all believers, regardless of age, gender or how new or old they are in their relationship with Christ!

Jesus promised *three* outcomes to *any* believer who would meet His one condition. His condition? The command to *Abide* in His word. To believers who would abide in His word, Jesus promised that: (1) They would become His *true* disciples; (2) they would *know* the truth; and (3) they would be *set free* from their enslavement to the unrelenting taskmaster of sin. Whether you've been a believer for five minutes or five decades, you are guaranteed these amazing outcomes, *if* you will simply *abide* in His word! So, what does it mean to *abide* in His word?"

The Greek word used in this verse is *meno*, and it means, "to continue in; to *continually dwell* or *reside in (within a given place.).*" Abiding in Jesus' word means to continually dwell within His words, listening to the Holy Spirit as He brings them into your mind and apply them to your moment-by-moment walk through your day. It means prayerfully meditating on what He said, and then *living within* the attitudes, actions and behaviors His words prescribe. Simply stated, abiding in His word, means continually *hearing* what He said and *doing* it. Even a child can hear His words and do them! Of course this requires faith. Faith, to daily take the time to read and review what He said and faith to take His prescribed steps of action throughout each day. This kind of faith will be graciously supplied by the Holy Spirit as we abide in Jesus' words. That's why Paul could proclaim, "Faith comes by hearing, and hearing by the word of God." (Romans 10:17)

Additional References for Study: Jesus Speaks, *May 10;*
Greatest Words, *Belief and Faith in Christ (445-51)*

Statement of Christ

"Then Jesus said to those Jews who believed Him, 'If you abide in My word, you are My disciples indeed. And you shall know the truth, and the truth shall make you free.'" John 8:31-32 (NKJV)

In my own words	SPECKS	I will
	Sin	
	Promise (implied or stated)	
	Example	
	Command (implied or stated)	
	Knowledge	
	Spirit	

4 Love Jesus the Way *He* Wants to be Loved

Special Insight

At *the last super*, Jesus gives five amazing promises and a revelation to His disciples. Once again, the promises are conditional. He promises that people who will fulfill His condition will be: (1) Loved by the Father (in a special way); (2) they'll be loved by Jesus (in a special way); (3) that He will reveal, manifest or show Himself to them; (4) that He and the Father will come to them; and (5) they will make their abode (dwelling place or home) with them. So what is the condition? That they love Him the way *He* wants to be loved—by *keeping* (obeying) His commands. And therein lies His extraordinary revelation—He said, "Whoever has My commands and keeps them is the one who loves Me." This is one of the most life-changing revelations any believer will ever hear. It literally reveals God's *love language*.

When *we* think of love, we usually think of an emotion-based love or the emotional feelings that we associate with love. But in John 14:21, 23 and 24, Jesus reveals that loving the Father and the Son the way *they* want to be loved is *not* accomplished with an emotional love; but rather, is only accomplished with an *obedience* love. In other words, we love the Father and the Son, by *obeying* the commands and teachings of Christ! In fact, in verse 24, Jesus said, "He who does not love Me does not keep My words." He couldn't make it any clearer. Those who obey His teachings and commands love Him, and those who don't obey His teachings and commands *don't* love Him. Anyone who will love Jesus by obeying His commands and teachings, will receive His amazing promises of being loved in a special way by the Father and Son and they will experience true intimacy of Jesus and the Father as They make their home with him.

Additional References for Study: Jesus Speaks, *January 4*; Greatest Words, *Loving God, Loving Christ (110)*

Statement of Christ

"Whoever has my commands and keeps them is the one who loves me. The one who loves me will be loved by my Father, and I too will love them and show myself to them." ..."Jesus replied, "Anyone who loves me will obey my teaching. My Father will love them, and we will come to them and make our home with them." John 14:21,23 (NIV)

In my own words	SPECKS	I will
	Sin	
	Promise (implied or stated)	
	Example	
	Command (implied or stated)	
	Knowledge	
	Spirit	

5 Believe Jesus - That He is in the Father and the Father is in Him

Special Insight

Jesus commands us to Believe that He has the relationship with God the Father that He says He has. So why does He make such a command? The answer is that He wants to reveal the Father to us. Remember that He said, "No one knows the Father except the Son and those to whom the Son chooses to reveal him." (Matthew 11:27 NIV).

Amazingly, He has chosen to reveal the Father to all of His followers, including you and me! Jesus reveals the Father with His words and with His life. He wants you to know and believe that when you see His behavior, His loving, righteous, just and merciful actions, you are seeing the Father, with crystal clear perfection. He wants you to believe that when you hear His words that you are hearing the Father's words. When you truly believe that He is in the Father and the Father is in Him, you will crave seeing the Father live His life through Christ in every circumstance and action recorded in the Gospels.

In Jesus alone can you perfectly see the Father living His life on earth, doing His work and speaking His words. Your belief of this truth will cause you to honor the Son, just as you Honor the Father. Your heart will fall in love with both the Father and the Son, and you will desire to love them by hearing and obeying Jesus' commands and teachings.   This is why Jesus said, "If you really know me, you will know my Father as well. From now on, you do know him and have seen him." He also said, "Anyone who has seen me has seen the Father;" and, "The words I say to you I do not speak on my own authority. Rather, it is the Father, living in me, who is doing his work." (John 14:7,9,10 NIV)

As you obey His command to believe this wonderful truth, you will see the Father and the Son as they really are. If you are worried about whether or not you can truly obey this command and believe this revelation, let me assure that you can. You can, because it is His will and He has given you the Holy Spirit to give you the power to act in faith upon this belief. Once again, the key, is abiding in Jesus' words.

Additional References for Study: Jesus Speaks, January 21, October 21; Greatest Words, Jesus Relationship With the Father (55-60; Commands of Christ (206-17); Claims of Christ (14-22)

Statement of Christ

"Believe Me when I say that I am in the Father and the Father is in Me." John 14:11 (NIV)

In my own words	SPECKS	I will
	Sin	
	Promise (implied or stated)	
	Example	
	Command (implied or stated)	
	Knowledge	
	Spirit	

6 Stop Doubting and Instead…Believe

Special Insight

If you have ever struggled with doubts, don't panic, you're not alone. In fact, I've never met a Christian or read a biography of a Christian who didn't struggle with doubts from time to time. Even the disciples struggled with doubts before the resurrection. The night of His resurrection, Jesus appeared to all of His disciples except Thomas who wasn't with them at the time. When they told Thomas they had seen the Lord, he didn't believe them. He said, "Unless I see in His hands the imprint of the nails, and put my finger into the place of the nails, and put my hand into His side, I will not believe." (John 20:25 NASB). Eight days later, when Jesus appeared to Thomas, He gave him the command to, "Stop doubting and believe." Thomas, answered, "My Lord and my God!"

But Thomas wasn't the only disciple that struggled with doubt. Peter had the greatest moment of faith in his life when he stepped out of the boat and began to walk on the water. And yet, within moments, his circumstances changed when a strong wind kicked up. Peter's faith in Christ and His command was immediately replaced with doubt. He sank and cried out, "Lord save me." Jesus reached out to him and saved him and said, "You of little faith, why did you doubt?" This points out that regardless of the faith you are exercising in one moment, in the next moment, a single change of circumstances can produce doubts that instantly replace your faith. The good news is, you can replace those doubts with faith, just as fast! All you need do is shift your focus from your circumstance, to the words of Christ. The Holy Spirit will then use those words to produce faith within you.

However, if you're not in the practice of abiding in Jesus words, The Holy Spirit's ministry of reminding you of what Jesus said may be severely limited. On the other hand, if you are consistently abiding in Christ's words, the Holy Spirit can quickly choose the words of Christ you need that will instantly replace your doubts with faith. Often times He does this by bringing one of Christ's commands to mind, and then by faith, you can obey that command. In His command to Thomas, Jesus made it very clear that He does not want us to linger in doubt and He doesn't want doubt to linger in us. So Jesus command to Thomas to stop doubting and start believing is just as applicable to us as it was to him. Whenever you find yourself being lured into doubt, immediately run to the words of Jesus. His words are spirit and life, and as Paul declared, "Faith comes by hearing, and hearing by the word of Christ." (Romans 10:17 NASB). Remember, doubts are mental, but faith is a choice—a choice to hear Christ's words in the moment, a choice to believe in that moment, and a choice to exercise faith in that moment by doing what He says. That is what He calls us to do!

Additional References for Study: Jesus Speaks, January 24; Greatest Words, Faith (231-37)
Anxiety, Worry and Fear (190-93)

Statement of Christ

"Stop doubting and believe." John 20:27 (NIV)

In my own words	SPECKS	I will
	Sin	
	Promise (implied or stated)	
	Example	
	Command (implied or stated)	
	Knowledge	
	Spirit	

7 Don't be Afraid, Instead Believe

Special Insight

As Jesus was walking with Jairus to his home, Jairus' friends came to him and told Jairus that it was too late—his twelve-year old daughter had died. As soon as he heard those words, he was overcome with fear and grief. His daughter was gone. He would never again hear her sweet voice. He would never hear her call his name or kiss her goodnight. He was devastated beyond expression. And then came the words that he never expected to hear—an instructive command that seemed to ignore everything he had just been told. Jesus gave him a simple word—a gentle command. He said, "Don't be afraid; just believe." Now, Jairus faced a choice…does he believe his friends and act on their advice to not bother Jesus with this any longer; or does he ignore their advice and instead believe Jesus by choosing to *act* upon His command. Jairus chose to believe Jesus and continued walking to his house. Little did he know, that his one act of simple obedience to Jesus' command would save the life of his precious little girl.

This command is as much for you and me as it was for Jairus.   You see, fear and faith are opposites. It's impossible to act upon both at the same time. They are just as opposite, as going up in an elevator is opposite of going down. You can't do both at the same time. You have to choose between up and down. Fear and faith can't govern your mind and heart at the same time. Fear is like a thermometer. It tells you that you are not trusting Christ. You need to quickly acquire the faith you need to follow Jesus in that circumstance. And you can't increase your faith by the power of positive thinking or chanting, "I believe, I believe, I believe." When you find yourself afraid of anything, you need to run to Jesus' words! They alone can produce faith when you are lacking it. Find His words that apply to your situation. Then choose to believe those words by doing what they say. *That* is choosing faith instead of fear! When you remain in fear, it's because you are choosing to ignore or the words of Christ or disobey them.

One night as Jesus and the disciples were sailing across a lake, a fierce gale arose and the waves began crashing into the boat. As the boat begin to fill with water, the disciples panicked. They awoke Jesus from His sleep, saying, "Teacher, don't you care that we're going to die?" (Mark 4:38 ISV). Jesus got up and then stopped the wind and calmed the sea with a single command, "Peace be still." He then said to His disciples, "Why are you so afraid? Do you still have no faith?" (Mark 4:40 NIV). You see, even though His own disciples had enough faith in Christ to leave everything they loved in life to follow Him, in *this* moment, they had let their fear replace their faith.   Friend, no matter how strong you may be in your faith in Christ, realize that at any given moment a change of circumstances can instantly produce fear that replaces your faith. That's the bad news. The good news is, you can replace that fear with faith as soon as you find a word or command from Christ and chose to act on it. And the more you get to know Him and His word, the easier it will be to act upon His command from Mark 5:36, "Don't be afraid, just believe."

Additional References for Study: Jesus Speaks, May 18; Greatest Words, Faith (231-40)

Statement of Christ

"Don't be afraid; just believe" Mark 5:36 (NIV)

In my own words	SPECKS	I will
	Sin	
	Promise (implied or stated)	
	Example	
	Command (implied or stated)	
	Knowledge	
	Spirit	

8 Running to Jesus Every Day

Special Insight

This command is certainly the most loving, the most kind, and the most beneficial command ever given in the history of mankind. To the unbeliever, it's more of an invitation—one with amazing promises given to those who come and take Him up on His offer. To the believer, this is not an invitation—it's a daily command! But it is a loving command. And provides these same wonderful promises to believers who will obey the command to "Come to Me," and the two other commands given in the remainder of the statement, namely, *harnessing* yourself to Christ and *learning* from Christ.

Here, His command is that you come to Him, and the implication of that command, is that you come to Him *first*. Whenever you are stressed, worried, fearful, panicked, terrified, overwhelmed, discouraged, depressed or defeated before you go to anyone else, go to Christ and His words.   His words are so reliable, He said, "Heaven and earth will pass away, but my words will never pass away." Matthew 24:35 (NIV). Are the words of anyone else as sure and reliable as that? Of course not. When you go to Him first, then you can look at everything from His point of view. He wants you to come to Him before you call a friend, a therapist, a minister or a relative, an author or any other person.

Take a moment and recall the last time you were worried, stressed or overwhelmed. Who did you run to? What did you do? Imagine the difference if you had run to Jesus and He had sat you down and told you the best way to handle it—what to do and the right approach and attitude for doing it. That's what He will do if you will study His words. Jesus wants you to get into the daily habit of running to Him, the moment you realize that you are weary or carrying a load. You run to Him by running to His words—they will not only give you the answers you need, they will infuse His spirit and life into your spirit and life.

But there's another step you can take. Turn to Matthew, Mark, Luke or John and look at His life, His experiences and His interactions with others. Ask the Holy Spirit to help you to begin to imitate Him in your attitudes and actions. In His life. He provides the perfect example of How the Father wants you and me to act! So we gain His instructions in His words and His example in His life.

Additional References for Study: Jesus Speaks, January 11; Greatest Words, Coming to Christ (452-3)

Statement of Christ

"Then Jesus said, "Come to me, all of you who are weary and carry heavy burdens, and I will give you rest." Matthew 11:28 (NLT)

In my own words	SPECKS	I will
	Sin	
	Promise (implied or stated)	
	Example	
	Command (implied or stated)	
	Knowledge	
	Spirit	

9 Harness yourself to Christ

Special Insight

Jesus calls all believers to "follow Me." We fulfill that command when we *hear* and *do* what He says. But here, He gives us a new picture. He tells us to come even closer...close enough that we can put His yoke on our shoulders. Most people want to "harness" others to themselves so they can get the help they need to carry their load. Not Jesus. Here he reveals that His intention is just the opposite. Instead of wanting us to bear a portion of *His* load, He wants us to be harnessed to Him so He can carry the full weight of *our* load!

He wants to carry even our heaviest loads that weigh us down so much that without Him, we can barely move. He wants to carry the loads that create our stresses, worries, fears, discouragements and despair. He will literally carry the entire load. All we have to do is harness up to Him and walk with Him, step by step. When we harness ourselves to Him, not only will He bear our burdens, He will guide us in the direction we should go, and show us which paths to take.

Talk about stress-free living, this is a solution no one else can give. We harness ourselves to Him by embracing all that He values and turning our back to that which He shows to be contrary to His values and purposes. The only way to know what He values once again, is to hear His words and do them, and imitate His life. Doing what He says is the very yoke or harness that ties us together. If we ignore or reject His words, we are rejecting the harness He offers. And when we reject His wonderful harness, we end up carrying our heavy load all by ourselves.

> Additional References for Study: Jesus Speaks, January 12; Greatest Words, Coming to Christ (452-3)
> Jesus' Words, Their Role and Power (62-64)

Statement of Christ

"Take my yoke upon you and learn from me, for I am gentle and humble in heart, and you will find rest for your souls". Matthew 11:29

In my own words	SPECKS	I will
	Sin	
	Promise (implied or stated)	
	Example	
	Command (implied or stated)	
	Knowledge	
	Spirit	

10 Learn from Christ

Special Insight

This third command found in Matthew 11:28-30 not only reveals the key to putting on Jesus' harness, it reveals the reasons why it is to our advantage to do so. The command is that we *learn* from Christ. He reveals that He is the absolute best teacher, leader, counselor and mentor that we could ever find. Why? First and foremost, He knows ALL of the truth! No one else who ever lived can make that claim. In fact, He not only knows the truth, He *is* the truth! (John 14:6). He alone can reveal the perfect truth to us, moment-by-moment, day by day.

Second, He's the absolute best because He is gentle and humble in heart. He teaches with a love that can be found in no other. Third, He's better than any other teacher or counselor because He carries the weight of our load! So we can rest—not just mentally and emotionally, but right down to our very soul! And when you have peace in your soul, you have true peace—peace that brings an incomparable rest and relief from your burden. He's the only counselor in the world that not only teaches you in spirit of gentleness and humility, but also offers to carry your burden!

Visualize going to visit with a human counselor. After sharing all of your problems, heartaches, fears, and sorrows, imagine that your counselor said, "Not only will I show you the answers to your problems, I'm going to relieve you from the weight all of your problems, worries and fears, by carrying them for you" Of course, no counselor would ever do that. And yet, Jesus makes that kind of offer to you every day. And He makes it in gentleness, humility and love. But His offer is conditional. It's only available if you will wear His harness by learning from His words, and obeying their instructions. He has given you the Holy Spirit who gives you everything you need to understand His words and do them. Jesus does everything!

One Sunday I was preaching on this passage in Puerto Rico. Later that afternoon, my daughter and I went swimming in the ocean. I got caught in a rip tide, and no matter how hard I swam, I wasn't able to get any closer to the shore. I was swimming hard, but not moving at all! I soon exhausted all of my strength. I soon stopped swimming, and didn't even have enough strength to tread water. A close friend of mine, a 6'4" former lifeguard, was about 20 yards away. I knew I only had enough breath for a single cry for help. I was less than a minute away from drowning. I yelled his name, and my strength and breath were gone. He turned toward me and yelled back, "Relax…I'm coming." He quickly swam to me and then said, "Grab on to my arm and relax—completely relax." I could barely hold on to him, but he safely carried me to the shallow water. I walked a few yards to the beach and collapsed. I was safe! This is what Jesus wants from us. He wants us to harness ourselves to Him and let Him carry us home.

Additional References for Study: Jesus Speaks, January 12; Greatest Words, Coming to Christ (452-3)
Jesus' Words, Their Role and Power (62-64)

Statement of Christ

"Take my yoke upon you and learn from me, for I am gentle and humble in heart, and you will find rest for your souls. For my yoke is easy and my burden is light." Matthew 11:28-30

In my own words	SPECKS	I will
	Sin	
	Promise (implied or stated)	
	Example	
	Command (implied or stated)	
	Knowledge	
	Spirit	

11 Listen to Jesus

Special Insight

Jesus alone has the authority to identify those who are His sheep and those who are not. However, here, He tells us how we too can identify His sheep, and how we can know if we are in His fold. In other words, He gives us the identifying mark or characteristic of all of His sheep. If a sheep has that characteristic, he or she is in His fold—they belong to Him. If they do not have that identifying characteristic, then, according to Jesus, they are not His sheep—yet! The identifying mark or characteristic of Jesus' sheep is that they listen to His voice, and they follow Him. Listening to His voice is simply a matter of learning and paying attention to His words; and following Him is as simple as doing what His words tell us to do.

Remember, in Luke 6:46, Jesus asks, "Why do you call Me, 'Lord, Lord,' and do not do what I say?" (NASB/NIV).   Just as those who don't do what He says have no right to call Him "Lord," when they continue to ignore or reject what He says, they are not following Him. And if they are not following Him, (unless they turn around and begin to do so), they can't have the knowledge or confidence that they are His sheep.

> Additional References for Study: Jesus Speaks, January 31;
> Greatest Words, Following Christ (245-53)

Statement of Christ

"My sheep listen to my voice; I know them, and they follow me." John 10:27

In my own words	SPECKS	I will
	Sin	
	Promise (implied or stated)	
	Example	
	Command (implied or stated)	
	Knowledge	
	Spirit	

12 Listen and Understand *This*

Special Insight

Here, Jesus gives us the command to listen and understand a very important truth. A truth that He knows is critical to our relationship and fellowship with Him. A truth that even the most diligent "Scripture Scholars" of His day did not understand.   It's not what we eat that spoils us. It's what comes out of our mouth that spoils us. Outwardly, we can do everything that makes us appear to be righteous and good. But what comes out of our mouth reflects what is in our heart. And it's what's in our heart that can "spoil" or ruin us before God.

As far as God is concerned, it's of no value to clean up the outside if we don't clean up the inside. He said, "But the things that come out of a person's mouth come from the heart, and these defile them. For out of the heart come evil thoughts--murder, adultery, sexual immorality, theft, false testimony, slander. These are what defile a person; but eating with unwashed hands does not defile them." (Matthew 15:18-20 NIV). He later told the same scholars, "You are those who justify yourselves in the sight of men, but God knows your hearts; for that which is highly esteemed among men is detestable in the sight of God." (Luke 16:15, NASB).

Jesus wants us to listen and to understand, that God wants us to focus on letting His word clean up our hearts, because out of our hearts come all of the issues of life. (Proverbs 4:23). Jesus told His disciples, "You are already clean because of the word I have spoken to you." If we abide in Jesus' words, the Holy Spirit will use them to cleanse our hearts and minds and keep them clean. And out of a heart that is daily bathed in His words, our attitudes and behaviors that flow outward will be a clear reflection of Him. This is what He meant when He told the disciples, (John 15:3)

Additional References for Study: Jesus Speaks, May 27; Greatest Words, The Heart (374-78); Lust (385); Sexual Immorality (488)

Statement of Christ

"Listen and understand. What goes into someone's mouth does not defile them, but what comes out of their mouth, that is what defiles them." Matthew 15:10-11 (NIV)

In my own words	SPECKS	I will
	Sin	
	Promise (implied or stated)	
	Example	
	Command (implied or stated)	
	Knowledge	
	Spirit	

13 Abide in Christ

Special Insight

Earlier, we looked at the amazing revelation of Jesus' conditional promises to any believer who would abide in His word, even believers who were only minutes old in their faith in Christ. The promised outcomes are true discipleship, intimate knowledge of the truth, and liberation from our enslavement to the terrible taskmaster of sin.

Now, we go one step further, namely, "abiding in Christ." Abiding in Christ means to continually dwell in or remain in Him. How do we do that? Simply stated, we abide in Him by *hearing* His teachings and commands and *obeying* them. (John 14:21-24). There is no other way to abide in Him. By hearing His words and doing them, the Holy Spirit reproduces Christ's life in us and conforms (or molds) us into His image. In I John 2:5, speaking of Jesus and His words, the Apostle John said: "But whoever keeps (obeys) His word, truly the love of God is perfected in him. By *this* we know that we are in Him." (emphasis added).

In this passage, Jesus promised that you will bear much fruit and that you will glorify God, if you abide in Him and His words abide in you. He is speaking of the fruit that comes from a life of faith in Him and His words. As we believe His words to the point of *doing* them, we will be glorifying the Father by honoring and serving the Son in the very ways the Father wants us to serve and honor Him. The fruit of the Holy Spirit (Galatians 5:22-23) will be produced in us and will flow out of our hearts into the lives of others. And they will see Christ, His heart and behavior in us—and *that* brings great glory to the Father!

Additional References for Study: Jesus Speaks, March 25; Greatest Words, Fruitbearing (257-60

Statement of Christ

"Abide in Me, and I in you. As the branch cannot bear fruit of itself unless it abides in the vine, so neither can you unless you abide in Me. I am the vine, you are the branches; he who abides in Me and I in him, he bears much fruit, for apart from Me you can do nothing."   John 15:4-5 (NASB)

In my own words	SPECKS	I will
	Sin	
	Promise (implied or stated)	
	Example	
	Command (implied or stated)	
	Knowledge	
	Spirit	

14 Let Jesus' Words Abide in You

Special Insight

In John 15:7, once again we have conditional promises and two implied commands. The promises are; that our prayers will be answered, that we will bear much fruit, that we will glorify the Father and that we will prove ourselves to be Jesus' disciples.

The two conditions are that we abide in Jesus and that His words abide in us. Because Jesus wants all of His followers to be his disciples, bear much fruit and glorify the Father, we can safely assume that abiding in Him and letting His words abide in us, are implied commands to all of His followers.

We abide in Christ by hearing His words and doing them. The Holy Spirit brings them to our mind and we need to respond by applying them to our moment-by-moment walk through life. God's grace and our faith in Christ are the means by which we receive the spiritual power to obey His words. That fulfills His command to abide in Him.

His command to let His words abide in us is fulfilled as we hear, read and meditate in Jesus' words. As we do this, the Holy Spirit permanently embeds those words into our heart and mind. They will literally abide in us. The more of His words and teachings that we hear, read and meditate on, the more words and teaching the Holy Spirit will be embed in us.

Additional References for Study: Jesus Speaks, January 5, January 14; Greatest Words, Fruitbearing (257-60); Prayer (295-98

Statement of Christ

"If you abide in Me, and My words abide in you, ask whatever you wish, and it will be done for you. My Father is glorified by this, that you bear much fruit, and so prove to be My disciples."
John 15:7-8 (NASB)

In my own words	SPECKS	I will
	Sin	
	Promise (implied or stated)	
	Example	
	Command (implied or stated)	
	Knowledge	
	Spirit	

15 Follow Jesus Now

Special Insight

One of Jesus' disciples wanted to follow Him and take part in His ministry, but first, he wanted to go home and tie up some loose ends, most likely help out in his father's business until his father died and the business could be liquidated. He made a simple request to Christ, using an expression that was often used to signify such a circumstance. Knowing that the Lord knew that he wanted to follow Him, he said, "Lord, first let me return home and bury my father." Matthew 8:21 (NLT). How did Jesus respond to this simple request to postpone "following Him?" Jesus firmly replied, "Follow me now. Let the spiritually dead bury their own dead." What this young disciple had failed to recognize was that nothing was more important or more urgent than following Christ. And since nothing is more important or more urgent, for those who are Jesus' followers, those who are spiritually alive, **there is never a time and never a reason to postpone following Him**.

Can you imagine being that young man? Having the chance to begin to walk, converse and minister with Jesus, day after day, month after month? Could anything be more wonderful? And yet, he made a terrible miscalculation. He undervalued Jesus and Jesus' calling. He was willing to set aside the eternal impact he could make in the lives of others and instead, settle for focusing on a very temporary need of taking care of the family business.   He was willing to trade that which is eternal for that which is as temporary as a passing cloud.

Friend, Jesus makes the same offer to you and me. He's called us to be His disciples now! He's called us to abide in His words, now! He's called us to follow Him now! Let's not be so foolish or shortsighted for even a day. Today, those who desire to follow Christ are busier than ever. The demands on our time, energy and attention are relentless. But obeying this command to follow Him now, is eternally impactful from the very moment you obey!

Additional References for Study: Jesus Speaks, April 8; Greatest Words, Following Christ (245-53); Living in the Present (277-78)

Statement of Christ

"Follow me now. Let the spiritually dead bury their own dead." Matthew 8:22 (NLT)

In my own words	SPECKS	I will
	Sin	
	Promise (implied or stated)	
	Example	
	Command (implied or stated)	
	Knowledge	
	Spirit	

16 Abide in Him and Receive His Will

Special Insight

Here we see another set of amazing promises—four miraculous outcomes: (1) You can ask for whatever you want, and it will be done for you; (2) the Father will be glorified; (3) you will bear much eternal fruit; and, You will prove yourself to be Jesus' disciple!

However, once again, these promises are conditional. You must fulfill two conditions to receive these promises. Not one, and not one-hundred. Only two.

1. You must abide (continually dwell) in Jesus, and

2. His words must abide (continually dwell) in you.

You abide or live within Christ by hearing and doing what He teaches and commands in His words. And His words actively remain in you as you meditate on them. It's not that complicated, and yet most professing believers do not abide in Christ, nor do His words abide in them. Abiding in Jesus' words are the very condition required to become one of His disciples. When you truly abide in Christ, you will find His will becoming *your* will, and His desires will become your desires—so you find yourself asking for what *He* wants. And He will joyfully then give you the desires you ask for. May the Lord open your eyes and your heart to this wonderful, glorious truth.

Additional References for Study: Jesus Speaks, January 15; July 28; Greatest Words, Prayer (295-298); God's Will (106-107)

Statement of Christ

"If you abide in Me, and My words abide in you, ask whatever you wish, and it will be done for you. My Father is glorified by this, that you bear much fruit, and so prove to be My disciples."
John 15:7-8 (NASB)

In my own words	SPECKS	I will
	Sin	
	Promise (implied or stated)	
	Example	
	Command (implied or stated)	
	Knowledge	
	Spirit	

17 Watch and Pray

Special Insight

In context, this command was given to the disciples when Jesus went off by Himself to pray, on the night of His arrest. But the principle behind this command is just as appropriate for you and me as it was for His disciples. Like them, our spirit is often willing to follow the Lord and obey His words, and yet, like them, our flesh is weak.

It's this weakness of our flesh that makes us so vulnerable to every kind of temptation and sin. We are often tempted to gossip, to envy, to covet, to be self-centered, to get angry, to be the lord of our own lives, and on and on. Even though we truly desire to follow Christ, our old nature has been so self-serving for so long, that we have little to no strength left to follow Him. That's the bad news.

The good news is, that in our weakness, Christ's strength is experienced and proven to the skeptical world around us. Jesus told the Apostle Paul, "My grace is sufficient for you, for my power is made perfect in weakness." And Paul's immediate response was, "Therefore I will boast all the more gladly about my weaknesses, so that Christ's power may rest on me." (II Corinthians 12:9 NIV). Of course, this goes hand in hand with Jesus' command in Matthew 11:28-29, to ""Come to me, all you who are weary and burdened, and I will give you rest. Take my yoke upon you and learn from me."

His command to "watch," is a command to "be on alert." In other words, don't slack off. We are living in a world that is ruled by the prince of darkness. He hates us and wants to do whatever he can to neutralize us and make us unfruitful for God's kingdom. He wants to do whatever he can to keep us from glorifying the Father and the Son and hearing the promptings of the Holy Spirit. Jesus is telling us to not be lulled in to falling asleep or becoming lazy in our efforts to follow Him. We are engaged in spiritual warfare, and therefore we must stay on alert and remain in communication with Him and the Father through our open channel of prayer.

Additional References for Study: Jesus Speaks, February 16; Greatest Words, Temptation (341-42);
Prayer (295-98)

Statement of Christ

"Watch and pray so that you will not fall into temptation. The spirit is willing, but the flesh is weak." Matthew 26:41 (NIV)

In my own words	SPECKS	I will
	Sin	
	Promise (implied or stated)	
	Example	
	Command (implied or stated)	
	Knowledge	
	Spirit	

18 Pray in Secret

Special Insight

In Jesus' day, the Pharisees and others loved drawing attention to themselves by praying loud enough to be heard by all who passed by. This is what Jesus was talking about when He said, "And when you pray, do not be like the hypocrites, for they love to pray standing in the synagogues and on the street corners to be seen by others. Truly I tell you, they have received their reward in full." (Matthew 6:5 NIV).

They will receive no answers to their prayers from God and their only reward will be the attention of others. After telling us not to be like these, Jesus tells us exactly how to pray in a way that God will hear our prayers and reward us. The reward will be His answer—one that will glorify Him; that which is in our best eternal interests and in the best interests of His kingdom and brings Him the greatest glory.

His very next statement was, "But when you pray, go into your room, close the door and pray to your Father, who is unseen. Then your Father, who sees what is done in secret, will reward you." Matthew 6:6 (NIV). You see, when we are alone and pray in secret, our prayer becomes all about Him and our relationship with Him. There will be no distractions and no appeal to our own ego or pride. This *doesn't* mean that we never prayer with others. As we will shortly see, Jesus encouraged His disciples (and us) to come together with one another and pray together. But praying with others is not the central purpose of prayer. It is a side benefit.

The central purpose of prayer is to have a time of transparency and intimacy with the Lord. We should be conversing with the Father throughout the day, wherever we are, whatever we are doing. But our daily conversations with Him should not replace the practice of setting aside time to get off by ourselves, closing the door and praying to Him in secret. Jesus didn't tell us this as a mere suggestion—it is one of His teachings and a gentle command that He wants us to obey.

Additional References for Study: Jesus Speaks, *February 5*; Greatest Words, *Prayer (295-98)*

Statement of Christ

"But when you pray, go into your room, close the door and pray to your Father, who is unseen. Then your Father, who sees what is done in secret, will reward you." Matthew 6:6 (NIV)

In my own words	SPECKS	I will
	Sin	
	Promise (implied or stated)	
	Example	
	Command (implied or stated)	
	Knowledge	
	Spirit	

19 Praying Together With Believers

Special Insight

Here, Jesus teaches His disciples the critical importance of coming together to pray in unified agreement. He makes two amazing promises to His followers.

1. In verse 20, He promises that whenever two or three come together in His name, committed to do His will together, *He* will come together with them and be right in the center of their fellowship.

2. He reveals that if those who are coming together and will have *agreement* (in their hearts), what they ask of the Father, He will do.

Throughout the ages, it has been debated whether this passage (which begins in the 18th verse) applies to all believers, or was Jesus was applying it only to His Apostles. I don't have the answer. But regardless, there are some very important principles that Jesus reveals here, that do apply to all of His followers.

First, this reveals that He truly wants His followers to come together and pray in agreement with one another. Second, He wants us to come together in His name—focusing our hearts, minds and souls on Him and His callings and purposes—seeking His will and doing it. While we may not be able to determine which side of the debate is right, we can obey His implied command to regularly come together with other believers, and in unity, worship Him, serve Him and pray. He wants us to *know* that when do this, He will be with us and we will have open access to the Father.

Additional References for Study: Jesus Speaks, December 17; Greatest Words, Prayer (295-98); Promises of Christ (298-304); Following Christ (245-53); Jesus' Name (51-53)

Statement of Christ

"Again, truly I tell you that if two of you on earth agree about anything they ask for, it will be done for them by my Father in heaven. For where two or three gather in my name, there am I with them." Matthew 18:19-20 (NIV)

In my own words	SPECKS	I will
	Sin	
	Promise (implied or stated)	
	Example	
	Command (implied or stated)	
	Knowledge	
	Spirit	

20 Don't Pray Like Superstitious Unbelievers

Special Insight

God is not like a human. He cannot be manipulated by flattery or ritual, no matter how religious the ritual may be. He doesn't judge a prayer or respond to a prayer based on how long the prayer is, how often it is repeated, or how flowery or poetic it may be.

God is not impressed by human wisdom or capabilities. In Jesus' day there were many who had adopted pagan concepts of prayer—that God would be more responsive to long prayers rather than short ones, or that if a prayer was repeated over and over again, God would be impressed with the efforts of the petitioner.

Here, Jesus once and for all dispels such humanistic and foolish notions. He commands His followers not to engage in such vain attempts to impress or manipulate the Father. The Father instead wants you to share whatever is on the top of your mind and heart until you have peace. He's not saying that you can't repeat your requests often, you can. But, His desire is that you share what's on your heart with Him, honestly and transparently with the intention of pressing toward more intimacy with Him.

Additional References for Study: Jesus Speaks, *February 27, 28, March 1,2,3;*
Greatest Words, *Prayer (295-98)*

Statement of Christ

"And when you pray, do not keep on babbling like pagans, for they think they will be heard because of their many words." Matthew 6:7

In my own words	SPECKS	I will
	Sin	
	Promise (implied or stated)	
	Example	
	Command (implied or stated)	
	Knowledge	
	Spirit	

21 Ask, Seek and Knock

Special Insight

In this passage from the Sermon on the Mount, Jesus gives His disciples (and us) the implied command to begin to do more asking of God, seeking from God and pursing opportunities to glorify God.   Evidently His disciples were slow to take the initiative in this area. Chances are, they had little confidence and found it much easier to let Jesus do all the work. Why ask God for anything, or seek anything from the Father, or seek out any opportunity to do more for God? After all, they were with the Savior—the one who could answer their questions and lead them into any opportunity without any initiative, effort or risk on their part. Jesus said as much about them two years later at the last supper when He said, "Until now you have asked for nothing in My name." (John 16:24 NASB).

Thankfully, everything changed when the Holy Spirit came upon them at Pentecost.

The great news for you and me is that God *wants* us to ask, seek and knock. He doesn't view us as a pest. He's not put off at all by any asking, seeking or knocking that we do. He loves us so much, He delights in it.   In fact, Jesus tells us that we will receive God's gracious gifts when we ask; He will let us find Him whenever we seek Him, and He will open His heart to us as we knock on it's door. Amazing Grace!

To emphasize this, Jesus gives us a wonderful picture that none of us can forget. He said, "Or what man is there among you who, when his son asks for a loaf, will give him a stone? "Or if he asks for a fish, he will not give him a snake, will he? If you then, being evil, know how to give good gifts to your children, how much more will your Father who is in heaven give what is good to those who ask Him!" (Matthew 7:9-11 NASB). Jesus is telling us all of this because He wants us to realize how much the Father loves us and how we can be safe with Him—He'll never demean us or reject us because of our requests.   No matter how loving, kind and patient our earthly fathers may be, God is infinitely more loving and kind.

Additional References for Study: Jesus Speaks, *August 31;* Greatest Words, *Prayer (295-98);*
Promises of Christ (298-304)

Statement of Christ

"Ask and it will be given to you; seek and you will find; knock and the door will be opened to you. For everyone who asks receives; the one who seeks finds; and to the one who knocks, the door will be opened." Matthew 7:7-8

In my own words	SPECKS	I will
	Sin	
	Promise (implied or stated)	
	Example	
	Command (implied or stated)	
	Knowledge	
	Spirit	

22 Pray Believing

Special Insight

This is a facet of prayer that is often overlooked or ignored.   And yet, when used the way Jesus intended, it can open up a channel through which God's blessings and miraculous answers to prayer can freely and abundantly flow. It's the ingredient in prayer that is often missing.

I'm talking about faith—the confident assurance that you will receive what you pray for. Abiding in Jesus' words will create and grow your faith faster than anything else you can do. When you hear His words and do them, the automatic outcome is the growth of your faith.   And when you add this kind of word-based, heart-based faith to your prayers, you will receive what you pray for.   I'm not talking about psyching yourself up or the power of positive thinking—I'm talking about faith that is truly birthed and nurtured by hearing the commands and conditional promises of Christ—obeying the commands and fulfilling the conditions. As you do that, your heart will be conformed to His heart, and your desire for the Father's will will increase and your desire for your will, will decrease.   And when you add this word-based, heart-faith to your prayers, nothing will be impossible to you!

A word of warning: When your prayers aren't answered the way you prayed that they would be answered, there are some people who will tell you, "you just didn't have enough faith." Or, you might quickly make the same judgment about yourself. Don't listen to such judgmental words from others, or from yourself. NO ONE has the right, the authority or the ability to Judge why or why God responds the way He does. Often times, God says "no" or "not now," not because there is a lack of faith or trust, but because He has a purpose, plan or outcome that better serves His eternal purposes than your petitioned request.

Additional References for Study: Jesus Speaks, *November 23;* Greatest Words, *Prayer (295-98);*
Promises of Christ (298-304); Faith (231-37; 445-51)

Statement of Christ

"Therefore I tell you, whatever you ask for in prayer, believe that you have received it, and it will be yours." Mark 11:24 (NIV)

In my own words	SPECKS	I will
	Sin	
	Promise (implied or stated)	
	Example	
	Command (implied or stated)	
	Knowledge	
	Spirit	

23 The Father *Wants* to Give the Holy Spirit

Special Insight

Here God gives us another amazing promise—greater than we or even His disciples could have imagined. The Father will not only give good gifts to believers who ask Him, He will give us the greatest gift any believer could ever receive—the Holy Spirit!

Imagine, God giving us access to Himself through the Holy Spirit. By giving us the Holy Spirit, He is giving us access to all of the unimaginable *ministries* of the Holy Spirit, and the selfless *fruits* of the Spirit (including God's agape love) and the *gifts and manifestations* of the Holy Spirit. While most believers are fully aware of the fruits and gifts of the Holy Spirit that Paul revealed in his epistles, Jesus identified twelve ministries of the Holy Spirit that are critical to the believer's life, their relationship with God, and their ministry. These ministries are:

1. Giving Spiritual Birth   John 3:5-8
2. Glorifying Christ by Revealing His Heart, Mind and Will to Believers. John 16:14-15
3. Teaching Us All Things and Bringing to Our Memory Everything Jesus Said   John 14:26
4. He Will Guide Us Into All Truth. John 16:13
5. Testify of Jesus to Us and Through Us. John 15:26-27 (NASB)
6. Be our Helper, Comforter and Counselor   John 14:16 (NASB)
7. Convict Unbelievers of Their Sin   John 16:8-9 (NASB)
8. Reveal the Righteousness of Christ   John 16:8-10 (NASB)
9. Reveal the Condemning Judgment of Satan. John 16:11 (NASB)
10. Reveal Future Events to Believers. John 16:13 (NASB)
11. Empower Believers With Spiritual Power   Acts 1:8 (NIV)
12. Empower Believers to Become Powerful Witnesses of Christ. Acts 1:8

Additional References for Study: Jesus Speaks, *February 19;* Greatest Words, *God's Goodness (97-99):*
Promises of Christ (298-304);The Holy Spirit (116-17)

Statement of Christ

"If you then, though you are evil, know how to give good gifts to your children, how much more will your Father in heaven give the Holy Spirit to those who ask him!" Luke 11:13

In my own words	SPECKS	I will
	Sin	
	Promise (implied or stated)	
	Example	
	Command (implied or stated)	
	Knowledge	
	Spirit	

24 A Commanded Prayer Request From Jesus

Special Insight

When was the last time you asked the Father to send out more workers into His harvest field? This is a teaching and a command of the Lord Jesus, and He doesn't want us to set it aside, not even for a single day. Jesus wants us to look at the opportunity to reach the world with His Gospel as a farmer looks at a harvest. When the crops are ripe, whether they be the fruit of the vine, the fruit of trees, or fields of wheat, the crop must be harvested within a limited amount of time, or the opportunity to harvest the crop will be lost. The world is filled with people who need to know Christ, and their time on earth is extremely limited.

People live in never-ending stress. They are confounded by fears and many hearts are full of despair. For example, in America, *suicide* is the number two cause of death for teenagers. Although many people love darkness rather than light because their deeds are evil, there are *many* whose hearts are longing for joy and peace. Many are being softened and prepared for harvest by the Holy Spirit. And yet, the workers who will reap the harvest are fewer than ever. That is why Jesus commands us to pray that the Lord of the harvest will raise up new workers every day, every week who will take the Gospel to the world and into the world around them. Will you obey this selfless command of Christ to pray that the Father would raise up and send forth more and more laborers into the Harvest? Will *you* be the *answer* to the prayers of others and become a reaper in this harvest as well?

As I write this, I want you to know that I have not been nearly as obedient to the Lord's commands and teachings on prayer, as He wants me to be. I have no strength or confidence in myself, only in Him, His grace and His mercy. I know that I must rely wholly upon His strength and upon the Holy Spirit for growth in my prayer life and in every area my life. That being said, I also have to tell you that I have had 50 years of answered prayers. I've seen miracles that I couldn't have even imagined or hoped for. I have seen His great, unmerited blessings so numerous that it would take a lifetime to recount them.   I've had many prayers answered with a "no" or with a "not now," or with a completely different answer than I prayed for. Some of His answers I have not understood, and at the time, didn't like. But most of the time, when He has answered with a "no" or a "not now," He provided an answer that was infinitely better than what I requested. And sometimes it took months or even years, to see how much better His answer was than my puny, short-sided request.   I am so glad that He is God and I am not. He amazes me with His grace and mercy, every day. Every day! Oh what a Father! Oh what a God!

Additional References for Study: Jesus Speaks, *June 16;* Greatest Words, *Diligence,
Sowing and Reaping (219-21); Prayer (295-98)*

Statement of Christ

"The harvest is plentiful, but the workers are few. Ask the Lord of the harvest, therefore, to send out workers into his harvest field." Luke 10:2 (NIV)

In my own words	SPECKS	I will
	Sin	
	Promise (implied or stated)	
	Example	
	Command (implied or stated)	
	Knowledge	
	Spirit	

25 Fear God, Then You Won't be Afraid

Special Insight

Solomon wrote, "The fear of the LORD is the beginning of wisdom." Today, people are quick to say that the Biblical phrase, "Fear God," merely means to *revere* God. They are half-right. Both the Hebrew and Greek words that are translated, "fear" when referring to God, encompass *both* reverence and terror. This kind of fear for God is not only the beginning of wisdom it is the very foundation upon which an intimate relationship with Him is built. It is this kind of "fear" that motivates us to want God as our Shepherd, rather than our enemy.

In Jeremiah 9:24, God described Himself as a God of love, justice and righteousness. There are two types of fear—good fear and bad fear. Good fear keeps us safe. When we are driving in a snowstorm, we slow down because we don't want to injure ourselves or others. That's good fear. Bad fear, on the other hand, paralyzes us and can keep us from doing what is best for us and those we love.

Fearing God gives us a desire to learn His boundaries that He has established—boundaries that reflect His eternal values and are in our best interests and the best interests of God and His kingdom. That same fear motivates us to set our focus on remaining within His boundaries. And as we realize that our sins have taken outside of His boundaries, subjecting us to His eternal judgment and condemnation, our fear of His judgment creates a desperate desire to be rescued from such a terrifying destiny. *Then,* when we see God's amazing, loving provision for our sin, this same fear motivates us to run to the Cross and joyfully accept the sacrifice that Jesus made to pay our debt and save us from our well-earned judgment. As we see God's incomparable love for us at Calvary, our hearts are filled with love for Him and gratefulness. We become even more amazed and grateful as we realize the greatness of our salvation and understand that God has removed our sin and clothed us in Christ's righteousness. The more we understand His holiness and our redemption, the more we revere and love Him.

The Key To a Fear-Free Life

The great news about this passage (Matthew 10:28-31), is that when we truly fear God, Jesus tells us we *won't* have to be afraid of anyone else, or even the Father. Even though this sounds like a contradiction, it is not. Because, when you truly fear God, you will run to Christ. And as you come to Him, He promises He will never cast you away. Instead, He will take you into His hands and you will see and know the Love of the Father. As you believe what He said, you will know your worth to the Father, and you won't have to be afraid. Remember, it is the Father who loves you so much that He sacrificed His only begotten Son for you!

Additional References for Study: Jesus Speaks, *April 14;* Greatest Words, *Anxiety, Worry and Fear (190-93)*

Statement of Christ

"Do not be afraid of those who kill the body but cannot kill the soul. Rather, be afraid of the One who can destroy both soul and body in hell. Are not two sparrows sold for a penny? Yet not one of them will fall to the ground outside your Father's care. And even the very hairs of your head are all numbered. So don't be afraid; you are worth more than many sparrows." Matthew 10:28-31 (NIV)

In my own words	SPECKS	I will
	Sin	
	Promise (implied or stated)	
	Example	
	Command (implied or stated)	
	Knowledge	
	Spirit	

26 Only Worship and Serve the Lord

Special Insight

After Jesus had just fasted for forty days and nights, Satan tried to tempt Him by offering Him all of the kingdoms of the world. All he asked was that Jesus would bow down and worship him. Jesus answered Him by quoting the Word of God. He said, "You shall worship the Lord your God, and Him only you shall serve." From a human point of view, it didn't seem like Satan was asking that much. If Jesus would just a give him a single bow and a moment of worship, he would give Jesus all of the kingdoms of the world. Jesus could have made a quick rationalization and justified such a seemingly insignificant gesture. But He didn't! Why? Most important, worshiping anything or anyone other than God would not have been an insignificant gesture. It would have been breaking God's highest law. It would have been an inexcusable violation of the Father's intimate union with the Son. Jesus would have committed the worst sin imaginable, and our salvation would have been forever lost. Jesus didn't fall for Satan's offer, because Jesus is the the light of the world. His light exposed Satan's offer for what it truly was—a deadly allurement to sin. But because Jesus is the light, Jesus saw it for what it really was—a simple lie that would have changed the destiny of all mankind.

Because Jesus submitted to the command of the Father to only worship and serve God, we can correctly deduce that this command applies to us as well. When we first consider this command, we may be quick to say, "No problem on this one, He's the only God I worship and serve." Unfortunately, a quick examination of how we spend your time and money might reveal otherwise. An examination of our priorities might uncover "gods" that we serve and even worship more than we serve and worship Him. We may have replaced Him on the throne of our hearts with money, material things, social status, work or even people that we love. And if we haven't been consistently abiding in Jesus' words, we may be clinging to countless idols that don't *seem* like idols at all. We are extremely vulnerable to the lies of Satan and the values of this world. Instead of seeing everything as God sees it, we may have seen everything as man sees it, embracing counterfeit values, truly believing they are real and perfectly okay.

Knowing this, when it comes to who or what we worship and who or what we serve, it's critical that we walk in His light. In the light of His words, we can keep things or others from replacing God on the throne of our hearts. Jesus said, "No one can serve two masters. Either you will hate the one and love the other, or you will be devoted to the one and despise the other. You cannot serve both God and money." (Matthew 6:24 NIV). Choosing the master of your life isn't a one-time decision. It's a decision that you make throughout your day. As you walk by faith, choosing to listen to His words and do them, He will remain on the throne of your heart!

Additional References for Study: Jesus Speaks, *April 27;* Greatest Words, *Commands of Christ (206-17)*

Statement of Christ

"You shall worship the Lord your God, and Him only you shall serve." Matthew 4:10 (NKJV)

In my own words	SPECKS	I will
	Sin	
	Promise (implied or stated)	
	Example	
	Command (implied or stated)	
	Knowledge	
	Spirit	

27 Worship God in Spirit and in Truth

Special Insight

Soon after Jesus began to talk with the Samaritan woman at the well, she perceived Him to be a prophet and asked Him a question about who was right when it came to worshiping God—her ancestors who said worship should be conducted on a particular mountain, or the Jews who said it should be conducted in Jerusalem. In essence, Jesus replied that when it came to worship, it wasn't the place of worship that mattered—it was *Who* was worshiped and *how* He was worshiped. He said, "You Samaritans worship what you do not know; we worship what we do know, for salvation is from the Jews." (John 4:22 NIV).

Worshiping God in Spirit and in truth is how God wants to be worshiped. Ascribing false notions to God, His nature, His person, His character or His purposes is not true worship. As we saw in Jeremiah 9:24, He wants to be understood and known for who He really is. He is a God of unfathomable love, a God of perfect justice and a God of absolute righteousness. He wants us to gain our glory by understanding and intimately knowing Him. To ascribe anything false to Him is to not know Him or worship Him in truth. Jesus said, "No one knows who the Son is except the Father, and no one knows who the Father is except the Son and those to whom the Son chooses to reveal him." (Luke 10:22 NIV). Jesus reveals the Father through the Spirit, through His words about the Father, and through His life. Therefore, it's critically important that we come to know the Father through the words and life of Jesus. As we do, we will worship Him in truth.

Worshiping God in Spirit, isn't about our emotional feelings; it's not about the songs we sing or about the words we speak. All of these things are wonderful and can be a part of our worship, but worship itself is that which brings *glory* to God in truth and Spirit, producing a heart and life that reflects a union with Him by *following* Christ. It's about worshiping Him with a heart that has been born again, transformed by the Holy Spirit that produces a life that is defined by denying yourself, taking up your cross daily and following Christ. That's why Paul wrote, "Therefore I urge you, brethren, by the mercies of God, to present your bodies a living and holy sacrifice, acceptable to God, which is your spiritual service of worship. And do not be conformed to this world, but be transformed by the renewing of your mind, so that you may prove what the will of God is, that which is good and acceptable and perfect." (Romans 12:1-2 NASB). No matter where you are in your worship today, you can begin to worship the Father in Spirit and truth today and everyday. Abide in the words of Christ, and everything else, (His rivers of living water) will then flow out of your relationship with Him. And the Holy Spirit will begin to mold your heart and your life into a heart and life like His.

Additional References for Study: Jesus Speaks, *July 21, July 20;* Greatest Words, *Worship (469)*

Statement of Christ

"God is spirit, and his worshipers must worship in the Spirit and in truth." John 4:24 (NIV)

In my own words	SPECKS	I will
	Sin	
	Promise (implied or stated)	
	Example	
	Command (implied or stated)	
	Knowledge	
	Spirit	

28 When You Obey Christ, Stay Humble

Special Insight

Pride is a little thing to us, but it is a very big thing to God. Humility on the other hand is a small thing to us, but a very big thing to God. Pride makes us think that we deserve praise and adoration for the good things we do, and makes us feel like we are more responsible for our achievements than God is. Pride makes us "spread our wings," and strive for independence from God. Humility recognizes that God and others are responsible for every good thing in our life. Paul said, "What do you have that you did not receive? And if you received it, why do you boast as if you had not received it?" You see, the truth is, even when we think we are independent from God, we are not. We are totally dependent on Him for everything—from our birth to our death. When we understand that truth, we become grateful beyond measure. When we don't understand that truth, we take credit for that which has been gifted to us by God, and lose all gratefulness.

Jesus knows that our very nature is to be arrogant. The person who thinks they aren't arrogant either doesn't understand arrogance, or they are the most arrogant of all. Arrogance is the father of all sin. It is the single greatest obstacle that prevents intimacy with God. When we are born again, we see ourselves as we really are and God as He really is, and in that moment, we become truly humble. However, because our old nature is so strong, Jesus knew that even as born again believers, pride would become an insurmountable obstacle to our fellowship with the Father, if it was not kept in check. So He gave his disciples a word picture that would be to them a constant reminder the Holy Spirit could use to help them remain humble. His word picture for them can be just as helpful to us. We want God's grace, not His opposition. And He promises grace to humble. Here's the word picture Jesus painted for His Apostles and us. "When a servant comes in from plowing or taking care of sheep, does his master say, 'Come in and eat with me'? No, he says, 'Prepare my meal, put on your apron, and serve me while I eat. Then you can eat later.' And does the master thank the servant for doing what he was told to do? Of course not. In the same way, when you obey me you should say, 'We are unworthy servants who have simply done our duty.'"

Your first reaction to this revelation and command may be like mine. I thought, "Wow, that's a little harsh." But it isn't harsh at all! Because if that becomes our attitude, God will flood our heart and life with His grace. But if that's not our true attitude, then we remain in arrogance, our intimacy with God is broken. Jesus gave His disciples and us this parable and command so that we could remain an empty vessel that could be *filled* with His grace! And out of His grace would flow rivers of living water. Oh what a Savior that loves us so much that He spotlights the truth, so we see can live and walk in His light.

Additional References for Study: Jesus Speaks, *May 31;* Greatest Words, *Humility (271-73); Pride (391-93)*

Statement of Christ

"In the same way, when you obey me you should say, 'We are unworthy servants who have simply done our duty.'" Luke 17:10 (NLT)

In my own words	SPECKS	I will
	Sin	
	Promise (implied or stated)	
	Example	
	Command (implied or stated)	
	Knowledge	
	Spirit	

29 Be Ready to Meet the Lord Any Minute

Special Insight

Can you ever remember a time when your boss was on vacation for a week or two? Wasn't that the best? Your stress level dropped. You likely didn't push yourself nearly as hard. Maybe you took longer lunches, spent more time on breaks and maybe even left work a little early. Let's face it, that is our nature. Thus, the saying, "when the cat's away the mice will play." And then comes the day when you know the boss will return the next morning. You become one lean, mean working machine. You clean up your workspace. You skip lunch and focus 100% on catching up all of your work so you're not humiliated by your boss saying, "What the heck have you been doing while I've been gone."

Now suppose your boss goes on vacation. But the day before he leaves, he tells you, "Here's what I want you to get done before I get back. It's critical, and if it's not done, there will be severe consequences." Then, he gives you terrible news. He says, "I don't know how long I'll be gone. I've got some issues here, so I could be gone for a couple of weeks, or I might even come home tomorrow night."

Now, how will you act while He is gone? Chances are you'll work just as diligently as you would if he was there. That is the message Jesus gives us with a number of severe word pictures in Matthew 24:36-50. Rather than me go through those parables line by line, you can do that on your own. They're self-explanatory. However, I will cut to the chase and spotlight the central command that Jesus puts right at the center of these parables: "Therefore be on the alert, for you do not know which day your Lord is coming." In other words, be diligent in your doing of what Jesus commands and teaches, moment-by-moment, day by day. Even though you cannot see Him by your side, be just as diligent as you would be if you *could* see Him by your side. After all, He has promised that as you obey His teachings, He and the Father will be with you. They will come to you and make their dwelling place with you. (John 14:23). How foolish we are when we behave as if He's not here and as if He never will be. These parables are focused on His appearing at His second coming, but they are just as applicable to us, even if He doesn't come tonight. For all of us are mortal. We are only one heartbeat away from death—from the end of *all* opportunity to serve Him on earth. Whether He returns to us, or we return to Him, we must heed this command. It will empower us to bear more fruit for Him, each day of our life.

Additional References for Study: Jesus Speaks *December 29*; Greatest Words, *Faithfulness (237-40)*; *Attitude (196-98)*

Statement of Christ

"Therefore be on the alert, for you do not know which day your Lord is coming." Matthew 24:42 (NASB)

In my own words	SPECKS	I will
	Sin	
	Promise (implied or stated)	
	Example	
	Command (implied or stated)	
	Knowledge	
	Spirit	

30 Give yourself to God

Special Insight

In Matthew 22:15-22, Jesus is approached by disciples of the Pharisees who try to trick Him into saying something that would cause Him to be charged with treason by the Roman authorities, or make Him viewed with hatred by His fellow Jews.

They said, "Tell us then, what is your opinion? Is it right to pay the imperial tax[a] to Caesar or not?" If he said, "Don't pay your taxes," he would be loved by the Jews and convicted as a traitor by Rome. If He said, "pay your taxes," He would be hated by the Jews but accepted by the Romans. There was seemingly no way He could win. But in God's grace and sovereignty, He not only won, He used the occasion to reveal a truth to His followers and give us a wonderful implied command.

He asked them for a Roman coin, and when the gave it to Him, He asked them whose image and inscription was on the coin. They of course replied, "Caesar's." His response dumbfounded them, and gave us a "coded message" with an implied command. He said, "So give back to Caesar what is Caesar's, and to God what is God's." (Matthew 22:21 NIV)

While this was the indisputable perfect answer (the only answer no one could find fault with) it was an amazing gift to us. Caesar's image and inscription on the coin meant the coin was created in Rome, by Romans and belonged to the Roman emperor.

My dear brother or sister in Christ, whose image and inscription is on you? From the very beginning of the Human Race, God revealed that we were created in *His* image. And when we were born of the Spirit, we not only became an adopted child of God, we took on His name! We bear His image, and His inscription is on *us*. Therefore, *we* belong to God, and we are called upon to give ourselves back to God, every day! The Apostle Paul wrote, "You are not your own; you were bought at a price." (I Corinthians 6:19-20.)   The price was His death on the cross! Oh what a Savior, oh what a God. I'm so glad He bought me back with the ransom of His life. What a joy to bear His image and inscription, and to belong to Him!

Additional References for Study: Jesus Speaks *April 30;* Greatest Words, *Spiritual Priorities (329-37)*

Statement of Christ

Then he said to them, "So give back to Caesar what is Caesar's, and to God what is God's."
Matthew 22:21 (NLT)

In my own words	SPECKS	I will
	Sin	
	Promise (implied or stated)	
	Example	
	Command (implied or stated)	
	Knowledge	
	Spirit	

31 Remember His Life and Death Every Day

Special Insight

As a youngster, I did not like the "communion" part of our church service. It seemed depressing and boring. I also didn't like singing every verse of Hymns or having to sit through long prayers. Needless to say, I see all of this in a very different light now. I still have a hard time with long prayers in a service and too many verses in a hymn or song. I have ADD (attention deficit disorder). So it's easy for me to lose my focus. However, I am so very grateful for the opportunity to partake in The Lord's Table, as it is referred to by many, Communion or the Sacrament by others. I know that Jesus commanded me to partake in this as a continuing reminder of the perfect life He lived and the terrible sacrifice He made to redeem *me*—one who is so undeserving of His grace and mercy!

This is no small deal to Him or the Father—it's a huge deal! Our redemption required that Jesus give up all of His glory in heaven and humble Himself more than anyone in history to become a mortal human. (See Philippians 2:5-11). The bread that represents His body also represents the perfect life He had to live every moment He was awake. And He lived that life to glorify the Father and to *qualify* as a perfect sacrifice that could redeem all who would believe in Him, repent and follow Him. That perfect life was broken like the bread and sacrificed for you and me!

And then there's His blood. You know that feeling of fear and panic that you get when you are bleeding? None of us would needlessly subject ourselves to a terrible injury where our blood would flow out of us without restraint or any hope of stopping. And yet, He willingly bleed for us. And *that* is what's represented as we drink of that cup. The bitterness of the wine or the unsweetened juice reminds us of the bitterness of Jesus' sacrifice—a sacrifice that was willingly given because of His love for the Father and His love for His sheep. And with His blood, He offers a new eternal contract to all who believe in Him. Oh that we might be obedient to this command, and remember Him every moment of every day. Oh How He loved us then—Oh how He loves us now!

> And when He had taken some bread and given thanks, He broke it and gave it to them, saying, "This is My body which is given for you; do this in remembrance of Me." And in the same way He took the cup after they had eaten, saying, "This cup which is poured out for you is the new covenant in My blood." Luke 22:19-20 (NASB)

Additional References for Study: Jesus Speaks, January 10; Greatest Words, Joy (273-75)

Statement of Christ

"do this in remembrance of Me." Luke 22:19 (NASB)

In my own words	SPECKS	I will
	Sin	
	Promise (implied or stated)	
	Example	
	Command (implied or stated)	
	Knowledge	
	Spirit	

32 Love Jesus *More* Than Anyone Else

Special Insight

This is one of the few statements of Jesus that use to wipe me out! I used to cry out to Him, "Lord, you know I want to love You more than I love my mom and dad, my sister, my wife and my kids, but you *know* I don't! You know my heart, so I can't even pretend that I love you more then them, because YOU would know it's a lie!"

Have you ever felt that way? I mean, think of how you feel toward your kids. Have you ever had that much love for Jesus? This use to weigh me down like no other verse in the Bible. It made me feel like I was a total failure in my love for God, and I knew that I had absolutely no hope of ever loving Him more than I love my children. Then, several years ago, as I was studying the words of Christ, everything changed! The light went on. I discovered how to love God more than I love my family. AMAZING! And before I knew it, I found myself doing just that—loving Jesus more than I was loving my wife and children. What happened? Did my feelings for my family decrease, or did my feelings for God increase? The answer is, NEITHER! I realized that when Jesus talks about me loving Him and the Father, He is *not* talking about the emotional feelings we call "love."   Loving Christ is not a matter of feelings, it's a matter of obedience! We love Him by *obeying* His teachings and commands. Look one more time at these excerpts from His statements in John 14:21, 23 and 24.

- "Whoever has my commands and keeps them is the one who loves me." John 14:21
- "Anyone who loves me will obey my teaching." John 14:23
- "Anyone who does not love me will not obey my teaching." John 14:24

These statements are so clear. When I'm obeying Christ, whether it's turning the other cheek, loving my enemy, forgiving someone who hurt me, etc., I am loving Him the way *He* wants to be loved. And when I do what He wants, even if it means I can't do something my family wants, then, I am loving Him more than I am loving my family.

We abide in the words of Christ, not to grow our feelings for God, but to grow our faith in Him and our express our love for Him by obeying His gracious commands. The more we meditate on His words, the more the Holy Spirit will be able to remind us of what He said. And the more He reminds us, the more faith we can exercise by obeying His words. The implied command of Matthew 10:37, to love Jesus more than one's own family, is now doable.   The great news is, *anyone* with the Holy Spirit can obey this command—a new believer or an old believer; a child, teenager, or an adult. And they can obey it without lowering their feelings for their family. All they need to know is, "What does Jesus want me to do in this moment," and then do it. And the more they abide in His words, the easier it will be to know what He wants! And when we do what He wants us to do in the moment or in a situation, we are loving Jesus and the Father more than we love anyone else, including ourselves!

Additional References for Study: Jesus Speaks, January 10; Greatest Words, Joy (273-75)

Statement of Christ

"Anyone who loves their father or mother more than me is not worthy of me; anyone who loves their son or daughter more than me is not worthy of me." Matthew 10:37 (NIV)

In my own words	SPECKS	I will
	Sin	
	Promise (implied or stated)	
	Example	
	Command (implied or stated)	
	Knowledge	
	Spirit	

33 Make Seeking God's Kingdom and His Righteousness Your #1 Priority

Special Insight

Because of my business, I do a lot of flying—dozens of flights and more than 150,000 miles per year. Before the flight leaves the ground, I usually ask the person in the seat next to me, "Do You live here, or there?" After they answer, I ask them "What do you do?" It's this question that produces interesting answers, especially with men. Of course, they always answer that question by telling me their occupation. They could just as easily answer, "I'm a husband," or "I'm a Dad." But they don't, because for most men, their work is their identity. In fact, they so identify with their work, that when men retire, it's common for them to lose their identity and become depressed.

How about you? Who are you? What do you do? What are you all about? James wrote: "What is your life? You are a mist that appears for a little while and then vanishes." (James 4:14). Our life on earth is merely a moment when compared to eternity—a single grain of sand on God's beach of time. And yet, Jesus tells us that even in this short life, we can store up treasures in heaven that are eternal! Is that amazing or what! We can actually do things in this life that will count for all eternity! Interestingly, I know how James would have answered my question, "What do you do?" He would have answered it the same way he started his letter—he would have humbly said, "I am a bond-servant of God and of the Lord Jesus Christ." That was his identity. Oh, that it would be ours as well!

During His sermon on the mount, Jesus gave a loving command to His disciples and to us when He revealed what He wanted our number one priority to be—the priority that would define who we really are and what our life would be all about. He said, "But seek first His kingdom and His righteousness, and all these things will be added to you." Matthew 6:33 (NASB)

How can you and I obey this command? How can we make our number-one priority, seeking the Father's kingdom, and His righteousness? Friend, the answer is so simple. We only need to follow Jesus—for in His words, we hear His moment- by-moment calling that leads us step-by-step into the Father's daily will for our life. And by looking at the Savior's life on earth, we see the perfect demonstration of God's righteousness, justice and love. To seek the Father's kingdom and righteousness, we only need to obey Jesus' commands and teachings and imitate His life. Wonderfully, as we harness ourselves to Jesus, He will carry our load—performing His righteousness in us and seeking the Father's kingdom through us. He is the vine and we are the branches. Oh what a Savior!

Additional References for Study: Jesus Speaks, *April 30;* Greatest Words, *Spiritual Priorities (328-37)*

Statement of Christ

"But seek first his kingdom and his righteousness, and all these things will be given to you as well." Matthew 6:33

In my own words	SPECKS	I will
	Sin	
	Promise (implied or stated)	
	Example	
	Command (implied or stated)	
	Knowledge	
	Spirit	

34 Store Up Treasures in Heaven - Not on Earth

Special Insight

This statement is where the rubber meets the road. For many (including the rich young ruler), this was and is "the line in the sand," that many of today's professing Christians will not cross. It really contains two commands. One "don't," and one "do." ALL of us have a strong attraction to material things and a powerful drive to acquire and treasure them. Unfortunately, many of the things we treasure reflect the values of the world rather than the values of God. When Jesus tells us to not store up treasures during our lifetime, He isn't trying to deprive us of something good, He's trying to free us of things that are worthless substitutes for those things that God values. Wonderfully, He wants us to receive something of far greater worth! So His first command in this statement is to get our heart "un-glued" from the treasures of the world. Gluing ourselves to the Father and Son provides greater riches, both for now, and for eternity! And those riches cannot be stolen or destroyed by any power on earth. After Jesus commands us to not lay up treasures on earth, He gives us the great news that we *can* acquire and store up riches in heaven, and He commands us to do just that. And the best news of all is this: As we store up those "heavenly treasures" our heart becomes glued to the Givers of those treasures—the Father, Son and Holy Spirit!

If you're like me, you're probably thinking, "How am I supposed to obey these two commands." First of all, Jesus is not saying you have to sell everything you treasure today, and give all the proceeds to the poor. However, the Holy Spirit may prompt you to do some pretty radical "simplifying" of your life. And I need to give this one caution. If you are married, whatever you decide to do with that which you treasure, you must not act unilaterally—but rather in unity with your spouse. You and your spouse co-own everything you have, and Jesus is not calling you to take away other people's treasures, (including those of your spouse and children.) He is talking about what *you* treasure. You must consider the needs of your family as well. Maybe the Lord will lead you together to sell a lot, or not sell anything. Maybe He'll lead you to give everything away, or maybe He'll lead you to give nothing away. As you begin to abide in Jesus' words, your cravings for the things and treasures of the world will decrease and your craving for God and what He values will increase!

The other side of this command is to START storing up treasures in heaven. How do we do that? As you follow Jesus by faith, obeying His commands and teachings, you will be storing up treasures in heaven that you are not even aware of. For example Jesus gave this promise to His followers: "And if you give even a cup of cold water to one of the least of my followers, you will surely be rewarded." Matthew 10:42. What you and I may view as even the smallest act of faith and obedience, will not go unrewarded. Oh what a God of mercy and grace!

Additional References for Study: Jesus Speaks, *May 13;* Greatest Words, *Wealth & Possessions (344-47); Spiritual Priorities (328-37)*

Statement of Christ

"Do not store up for yourselves treasures on earth, where moth and rust destroy, and where thieves break in and steal. But store up for yourselves treasures in heaven, where neither moth nor rust destroys, and where thieves do not break in or steal; for where your treasure is, there your heart will be also." Matthew 6:19-21 (NASB)

In my own words	SPECKS	I will
	Sin	
	Promise (implied or stated)	
	Example	
	Command (implied or stated)	
	Knowledge	
	Spirit	

35 Only Serve One Master - Don't Serve Money or Anything else--Only God!

Special Insight

Here again, Jesus draws the line in the sand and gives us a wake-up call. Very few of us would admit that we serve any master other than God, and even fewer would admit that money or wealth is the master that we serve. Fortunately, Jesus only tells the truth! Fortunately, He is the light of the world, and when He shines the light of His words into our heart, we can see everything in our lives as *He* sees everything. Serving money or wealth is a problem that we all have. It is as ingrained into our nature as much as chemical toxins are stored in the cells that we are made of.

Fortunately, we can rid ourselves of this spiritual toxin every day. Every day, empowered by God's grace, we can make choices that give God the lordship of our lives and dethrone money and wealth and any other master we find ourselves serving.

Do you know the 150-plus commands Jesus gave to His followers? How about His 100-plus conditional promises? How about His more than 100 revelations about His relationship with the Father, or His 170 divine claims about Himself? Do His thoughts fill your mind and His Spirit fill your heart? Are rivers of living water flowing out of you every day? Are you daily overwhelmed by His mercy and grace—by your knowledge of Him and your intimacy with Him? Are you daily rejoicing in the greatness of your salvation? Or are you troubled by stress, worries or fear?

My dear friend, the first step to becoming intimate with Christ and making God the Master of your life, is being honest about where you really are in your relationship with Him. Are you hungering and thirsting for His righteousness, or are you pretty complacent? Here's the Good News of the Gospel. Wherever you are right now, whoever or whatever you have allowed to be your master, everything can change in an instant! For God Himself wants intimacy with YOU! And you can make Him the master of life each day. How? By hearing His Son's voice and following Him. He is the only Master who will truly satisfy your every need and longing. He alone can give you His supernatural peace, joy and unselfish love.

Will you make Him your master? Choosing your master is not a once in a lifetime decision. It's a moment-by-moment decision we make many times a day. When you choose God, you are loving Him. Who or what will be your Master today? Tomorrow and the next day? Choose Him, Choose Him, Choose Him! All the angels of heaven are cheering for Him and they are pulling for you! He loves you so much!

Additional References for Study: Jesus Speaks, *February 3;* Greatest Words, *Wealth & Possessions (344-47)*

Statement of Christ

"No one can serve two masters. Either you will hate the one and love the other, or you will be devoted to the one and despise the other. You cannot serve both God and money." Matthew 6:24

In my own words	SPECKS	I will
	Sin	
	Promise (implied or stated)	
	Example	
	Command (implied or stated)	
	Knowledge	
	Spirit	

36 Lose Your Life in Christ

Special Insight

Before we encounter Christ, our *natural* drives and inclinations are all about ourselves and our self-interests. We do what we think will bring us the most benefit, pleasure and happiness. We try to get people to fit into our plans and do what *we* want them to do. Our natural desire is to be *served* rather than to serve. Our natural desire is for a god who will be a "Santa Clause" type god—one who serves us and gives us what we want. Our nature is to put ourselves *first* and God and others a very distant second. Jesus calls us to make a 180-degree change in the direction of our lives. The New Testament Greek word for *repent*, was a military command that meant to make an "about face." To repent means to change the direction of your life from one of doing your will, to one of doing *God's* will. "Denying yourself," means to set aside your self-interests to pursue the interests of God. It means saying "no" to your self-centered desires, and instead saying "yes" to God's desires.

When Jesus calls us to take up our cross daily, He is giving us a picture of a man who is walking through the remainder of his life carrying the very instrument of his death. Taking up our cross each day means *dying* to our own self-desires each day. But it also pictures more than that. A man carrying a cross has no "rights." But for the believer, with this death to self comes a brand new life. When we "choose" to take up our cross daily, we are responding to Christ's call to *yield* all of our rights to God and to submit to *Him* as the *master* of our life. Like a man carrying a cross, we have no *right* to happiness, health, prosperity, self-gratification, love, security or respect. We have no right to have others meet our needs and desires. But, as we die to self, we have the *promise* of a whole new life—one in which we live in an eternal relationship with the Almighty God.

We have the promise of finding a brand new life *in Him*. We have the promise of the eternal love of God and an *eternal* life that is more secure and indestructible than the heavens and earth. When we take up our cross, we have the promise of bearing much fruit in our life and in the lives of others—fruit that will please and glorify God. And when we yield all of our rights to God, we set aside all expectations and entitlements. So we view every benefit that comes our way as an unexpected, un-entitled *gift*. This creates true gratefulness that in turn creates true happiness and joy—a joy that will overflow to everyone who comes into our path. This is why Jesus could promise, "Whoever loses their life for My sake will find it." Matthew 10:39 (NIV).

The new life we find in Christ, is *His* life, and it flows into us from Him. We become a vessel of His never-ending stream of *living* water. Of the three callings here in Matthew 16:24-25, "follow Me," is perhaps the most simple and yet the most misunderstood. While He called only a few to travel with Him, He called *all* who would believe in Him to follow Him in a far more important way. *That* is the call He extends to you and me. In John 10:27, Jesus reiterated this call when He said, "My sheep hear My voice, and I know them, and they follow Me." Here the meaning of His call becomes perfectly clear. To *follow* Him, His sheep must *hear* His voice—they must listen to His words and follow Him by *doing* what He says. They must hear His voice, not once, but continually! Following Jesus is no more and no less than continually hearing His words and *doing* them—hearing His instructions, teachings and commands, and obeying them!

Additional References for Study: Jesus Speaks, *February 8;* Greatest Words, *Following Christ (245-53)*

Statement of Christ

"If anyone wishes to come after Me, he must deny himself, and take up his cross and follow Me. For whoever wishes to save his life will lose it; but whoever loses his life for My sake will find it." Matthew 16:24-25

In my own words	SPECKS	I will
	Sin	
	Promise (implied or stated)	
	Example	
	Command (implied or stated)	
	Knowledge	
	Spirit	

37 Don't Be Afraid, Even of Those Who Can Kill You

Special Insight

I once read that a survey revealed that public speaking was the number one fear of most adults. The same article said the fear of death was number six. That may have been true at the moment the people answered the survey—but I'm sure for most people, it all changes when they're about to die. Death will become their number one fear and all of their other fears will fade into insignificance.

So the question is, "How?... How can we conquer this greatest of fears and every other fear that we will ever encounter?" In Matthew 10:28-31, Jesus not only commands us to not be afraid of anyone or anything that can kill us. He tells us how to overcome such fears. He said:

> "And do not fear those who kill the body but cannot kill the soul. But rather fear Him who is able to destroy both soul and body in hell. (emphasis added).

> He then states: Are not two sparrows sold for a copper coin? And not one of them falls to the ground apart from your Father's will. But the very hairs of your head are all numbered. Do not fear therefore; you are of more value than many sparrows."

In this passage Jesus tells us exactly how we are to deal with the fear of death and people that can cause our death. First, realize that this fear and all fears (other than the fear of God) are the result of us focusing on and over-valuing that which is only temporary. For believers, even death is merely the conclusion of the very brief and temporary phase of our lives—our time on earth! It is a momentary doorway to our *eternal* home.

What else are you afraid of? The loss of money or material possessions? The loss of a job? The loss of a relationship? The loss of status? The Loss of respect? The loss of health? The loss of mobility? The loss of independence? All of these fears are also focused on losing that which is only temporary. None relate to anything that lasts beyond this life! So Jesus tells us to not fear the loss of anything that is only temporary. But How are we to do that? It begins by seeing all of these temporary things the way He sees them. They were never meant to be permanent possessions, but merely something God gave us for our brief time on earth.

Additional references for study: Jesus Speaks, *January 25;* Greatest Words, *Anxiety, Worry & Fear (190-93)*

Statement of Christ

"Do not be afraid of those who kill the body but cannot kill the soul." Matthew 10:28

In my own words	SPECKS	I will
	Sin	
	Promise (implied or stated)	
	Example	
	Command (implied or stated)	
	Knowledge	
	Spirit	

38 Be Courageous, Don't be Afraid

Special Insight

Here Jesus reveals that He not only wants His followers to not fear, He wants them to replace their fear with courage. He gave this revelation to His disciples one night when they saw Him walking on the water toward their boat. At first, they thought they were seeing a ghost and they were terrified! He was far enough away that they could not see Him clearly. In the original language, the Greek word that was translated into the phrase, "take courage," is always used in the imperative, meaning it was a command, not a suggestion or a request. Even though this was a stated command to His disciples, we can take it as an *implied* command to us. He's implying that it's not enough to "not be afraid," but He wants us to use the same faith it requires to overcome our fear to be courageous and act courageously.

Courage is not a feeling. Courage is a behavior and a choice. My dad was a B-24 bomber pilot in World War II. He flew 48 combat missions in the South Pacific. He was terribly scared every time He took off on a mission. And when His plane would be attacked by enemy fighters and by anti-aircraft fire from the ground, he was terrified. But, he still followed orders and took his plane up on 48 missions. He said that when fighters would be diving at his plane, they would come so close that He could see the faces of the fighter pilots. He was truly terrified. And yet, he would continue to fly in formation to the target.   In spite of his feelings of terror, he would exercise courage until his mission was completed and his plane safely returned to its base.

Jesus wants all of His followers, men, women, boys and girls to replace their fear with faith and courage.   Once again, the question is How? After all, when we're scared, we can't just close our eyes and wish for courage and have it automatically take over. In this wonderful command of Christ, He tells us how. He commanded His disciples, "Take courage," and immediately revealed how when He said, "It is I." You see, the key to acting courageously when you feel terrified is realizing that Jesus is present with you, even in that moment! And when He's with you, nothing is going to steal you away from Him, His care and His will for the absolute eternal best for you!

When you believe Him, you will act upon that knowledge, regardless of how scared you may feel. You will receive courage from Him to do what's right, even if you're terrified. And when you do this, you will be obeying His command to be courageous, and don't act in fear. You don't have to change your feelings! You just follow Him, one step at a time! It's your actions that express your faith, not your feelings—and God is pleased and glorified when you express your trust in Him by acting in courage instead of acting in fear.

Additional References for Study: Jesus Speaks, February 14; *Greatest Words, Anxiety, Worry & Fear (190-93)*

Statement of Christ

"Take courage! It is I. Don't be afraid." (Matthew 14:27)

In my own words	SPECKS	I will
	Sin	
	Promise (implied or stated)	
	Example	
	Command (implied or stated)	
	Knowledge	
	Spirit	

39 Don't be Afraid, Simply Believe

Special Insight

Jairus' twelve year-old daughter, his only child was dying. In grief and despair, he fell at Jesus' feet and pleaded with Him to come to his house and heal her. Jesus agreed to go with him, but before they could even get started, Jesus stopped because a woman hoping to be healed had touched His robe. While He was talking to her, Jairus' friends came from his home and told him that his daughter had died. They said, "Why trouble the Teacher" any further."

Can you imagine receiving such terrible news? His whole world was shattered. All hope was gone! And yet, at that very moment, our dear Savior gave Jairus a command—a command that is just as applicable to us today as it was for Jairus. Jesus said, "Don't be afraid; just believe." At that moment, Jairus had to make a choice. Does he believe his friends that his daughter was dead, that all hope was gone, and follow their plea to leave Jesus alone; or, does he listen to Jesus and obey His command to, 'Don't be afraid, just believe.'

Jairus could have easily said to Jesus, "What do you mean, 'don't be afraid, just believe?' Didn't you just hear what they said? It's too late! She's dead!" But Jairus didn't say that. Instead, he chose to obey Jesus' command to act in faith and do what He said—stop fearing and believe. Believe Jesus and walk with Him back to his home. And because He believed Jesus to the point of obeying His command to not be afraid, but to believe, the life of his precious little girl was revived. What a tragedy it would have been if he had decided to believe his friends and act on their advice instead of believing Jesus. He would have never had another minute with the love of his life.

What would happen with you, if every time a fear entered your mind, instead of lingering in that fear, you obeyed this command? You replaced that fear with action—choosing to believe Jesus and His words and act accordingly? You only have to believe Him, one step at a time, one moment at a time, and your faith will bear fruit that will glorify the Father.

Additional References for Study: Jesus Speaks, *May 17;*
Greatest Words, *Anxiety, Worry & Fear (190-93); Faith (231-40)*

Statement of Christ

"Don't be afraid; just believe." Mark 5:36

In my own words	SPECKS	I will
	Sin	
	Promise (implied or stated)	
	Example	
	Command (implied or stated)	
	Knowledge	
	Spirit	

40 Don't Worry About Tomorrow

Special Insight

Right now, think about one of your current worries or fears. Once you've thought about it, answer this question: "Is it a worry or fear about something that is happening right now (as you are reading this, or is it something that may happen in the future?) Remember, the future can be five minutes from now or five years from now. Now think of one more thing you are worrying about. Ask the same question—is that worry about something that may happen right now, or is it something that might happen in the future?

The truth is, I've never worried about anything that is in the present moment, and neither has anyone else. All worries and fears come when our minds drift into thinking about the future. The concerns that cause our worry reside in the future. When I worried that I might be fired after my lunch break, the possible firing I was worrying about was thirty minutes away…in the future. When I was about to be put under anesthesia for an emergency appendectomy, my worry about the pain I might experience after the operation, was in the future.   When I've worried about my possible failures in business, those possible failures were always in the future.

As you view Jesus' command to not worry about tomorrow (or anything in the future), it's only natural to think, "And how am I supposed to not worry about the future? I could be facing real trouble in the next few minutes/days/weeks or months." Well the good news is, Jesus tells us exactly how to not worry about the future. This command in Matthew 6:34 begins with the word, "therefore." In other words, the reason we should not worry about anything in the future, is the statement Jesus had made immediately preceding this one. It too was a command. He said, "But seek first his kingdom and his righteousness, and all these things will be given to you as well."

He said "seek," meaning do not be idle or passive, but passionately pursue God's kingdom and His righteousness. And He further qualified that with the word, "first." So put it all together and we have, "passionately pursue God's kingdom and His righteousness, and make the pursuit of His kingdom and righteousness, first and foremost above everything else in your daily life. And when you fill your *present* moments with the priority of pursuing God's kingdom and righteousness, you are not to let your worry of future events distract from that pursuit, nor pull your mind and heart out of the present moment!"

Additional References for Study: Jesus Speaks, *January 14;* Greatest Words, Anxiety, *Worry & Fear (190-93); Living in the Present (277-78)*

Statement of Christ

"Therefore do not worry about tomorrow, for tomorrow will worry about itself. Each day has enough trouble of its own." (Matthew 6:34)

In my own words	SPECKS	I will
	Sin	
	Promise (implied or stated)	
	Example	
	Command (implied or stated)	
	Knowledge	
	Spirit	

41 Don't Worry About Your Basic Needs

Special Insight

Do you ever stress about what you are going to wear? Do you ever stress or about your appearance? Ladies, how much time do you spend on your face, hair, or nails? Men, how much time do you spend trying to decide on a shirt or tie, or what you should wear for this meeting or that one? Do you ever worry about what you're going to eat for lunch or dinner? If you're having people for dinner, do you stress about what you're going to serve them?

Next time you go to a department store, take a stroll through women's clothing, women's shoes, and the makeup section. You'll see how serious most women are when it comes to choosing their clothes, shoes and makeup. The amount of time they take looking, trying on, and experimenting is significant. Any husband who has shopped with his wife, already knows this. Of course, you could see something similar with men when you walk into a car dealership, or a sporting good store. Go to any restaurant and watch how carefully everyone studies the menu. All said, we spend an awful lot of time, effort and stress focusing on things that do nothing to draw our hearts closer to God. I'm not saying that you shouldn't care at all or that you shouldn't be a wise shopper, I'm just saying we *often* spend more time and attention focusing on these temporal things than we do on meditating in the words of our dear Savior.

Imagine what would happen if we would spend the same number of minutes each week focusing on the words of Christ or serving Him in the ways He calls us to serve. Imagine what would happen if we would give as much attention to nurturing our relationship with God as we do focusing on that which is only temporal. Jesus isn't saying we should abandon everything temporal, He's "turning the light on," exposing that we spend too much time, attention, effort and stress on things that don't matter to God, and by comparison, spend too *little* time and attention focusing on that which is of eternal worth, to God and to us.

Here, Jesus simply commands us to stop worrying, or "stressing" about our basic needs. But He doesn't stop by telling us what not to do. He follows this statement with a statement that tells us what to do in its place. In the very next breath, (verse 33), Jesus says, "But seek first His kingdom and His righteousness, and all these things will be added to you." In other words, instead of spending so much time, effort and stress focusing on the temporal things, spend that time and effort focusing on and pursuing God's kingdom and righteousness. When you do this, you won't have to stress at all, because God Himself will then give you everything you need, *without* the worry or stress.

Additional References for Study: Jesus Speaks, *August 5;* Greatest Words, *Anxiety, Worry & Fear (190-93)*

Statement of Christ

"So do not worry, saying, 'What shall we eat?' or 'What shall we drink?' or 'What shall we wear?' For the pagans run after all these things, and your heavenly Father knows that you need them." Matthew 6:31-32

In my own words	SPECKS	I will
	Sin	
	Promise (implied or stated)	
	Example	
	Command (implied or stated)	
	Knowledge	
	Spirit	

42 Don't be Alarmed by Wars and Uprisings

Special Insight

Those of us who have studied Bible prophesy know that Revelation 9:15 prophesy's a world war that would begin in Iraq, in which one third of the world's population would be destroyed, (more than 2.4 billion people). Today, with the advent of rich and powerful Islamic terror organizations, starting such a war not only seems possible, it seems inevitable. And yet, Jesus commands us not to be afraid as we see the pre-cursing events taking place. How can He tell us not to be frightened as we see these terrifying events taking place? The answer can only be found as we embrace and truly believe His command to not be afraid of those who kill the body but cannot kill the soul.

The truth is, every human on earth today (including you and me) will ultimately die. (Other than those who are here on earth when Jesus returns.) And other than a few moments or minutes of pain, it doesn't make much difference if we die from a spear, an animal attack, a car accident or a nuclear weapon. For the believer, any means of death is no more than a "page turn" that ends the temporary chapter of our life, and begins the next chapter—the one that is glorious and eternal. And Jesus commands us to not let the fear of these "end-time" events distract or divert us from our calling to be His moment-by-moment lights in this dark world.

Once again, whenever we fear anything, we are living in the future, and missing the miracle of the moment. That's why the Apostle Paul tells us, "Therefore be careful how you walk, not as unwise men but as wise, making the most of your time, because the days are evil. So then do not be foolish, but understand what the will of the Lord is." (Ephesians 5:15-17 NASB). No matter what terrible evil surrounds us, Jesus commands us to live in the moment, and Paul tells us to make the most of the moments we're in. Like all of Jesus' followers who have preceded us, our mission is to follow Him and do what *He* wants, each day. And all of the worrisome events that surround us do not change Him, His call or our response to His call. Our brothers and sisters in the Middle East are being martyred because they are refusing to deny Him. We hate what Satan's armies are doing to God's precious ones. But their victory is but for a moment. The victory of Jesus' martyrs is an eternal victory filled with a glory that will never end.

Jesus knows that our immediate reaction to such terrible events is fear. He's not condemning our reaction, but He's telling us not to *linger* in that reaction—to turn our eyes back to Him as fast as we can. Instead of remaining in the fear that these events cause, rejoice that none of this is taking us by surprise— it was all clearly and perfectly prophesied in the Word of God. These events *confirm* our faith, they don't undermine or contradict it. Keep looking at our Shepherd—keep listening to His word. Remember that He said, "Heaven and earth will pass away, but my words will never pass away." (Matthew 24:35)

Additional References for Study: Jesus Speak, *February 22;* Greatest Words, *Anxiety, Worry & Fear (190-93)*

Statement of Christ

"When you hear of wars and uprisings, do not be frightened. These things must happen first, but the end will not come right away." Luke 21:9

In my own words	SPECKS	I will
	Sin	
	Promise (implied or stated)	
	Example	
	Command (implied or stated)	
	Knowledge	
	Spirit	

43 Don't Worry About Your Life

Special Insight

"What do you mean, don't worry about my life…do you have any idea what I'm going through?"

That could easily be the response of anyone who hears Jesus' command to not worry about their life. And yet, this is a command of Christ. And I know His love language is obedience to His commands. (John 14:21-23). So if I want to love Him the way He and the Father want to be loved, this is one more command I need to obey. But once again, the question is "How?" How am I supposed to not worry about my life, when it seems like there is so much to worry about?

Here, as in other places, we can find the key in the statement that immediately precedes this command, because once again, Jesus begins this command with the word, "therefore." So this command and obeying it are inextricably linked to the statement that preceded it. In that statement, (verse 24), Jesus said, "No one can serve two masters. Either you will hate the one and love the other, or you will be devoted to the one and despise the other. You cannot serve both God and money."

How does "not serving two masters" relate to "not worrying about our life?" The truth is, when we worry about our life and act out of that worry, we are making our life about ourselves. We are becoming the very master that we serve. We are replacing God as the master of our lives, with ourselves. You see, when He is the master of my life, my life is about Him and serving Him, not about me and serving me!

When I serve Him, He's in charge. When I serve Him, it's His mission and purposes that count, not mine. If they get interrupted by terrible circumstances befalling me, that's *HIS* business, not mine—His problem, not mine! If serving Him causes me any discomfort, pain or even my death, it's okay. For in this brief life, I now belong to Him. I am HIS sheep—I follow Him!

When you are worrying about your life or anything in or about your life, let that be like a red flag that tells you to turn your eyes back to Jesus. Listen to His voice and follow Him. Step off of that ruling throne in your life, and let Him have it back. Even if you have to do it a hundred times a day, do it every time you realize you are worrying. After all, how wonderful to have the almighty God who created the universe as your dear Shepherd and Master. He loves us with an infinite, eternal love that you and I can't even imagine. Remember He has told us, "I have told you these things, so that in me you may have peace. In this world you will have trouble. But take heart! I have overcome the world." (John 16:33)

Additional References for Study: Jesus Speaks, *August 5;* Greatest Words, *Anxiety, Worry & Fear (190-93)*

Statement of Christ

"Therefore I tell you, do not worry about your life," Matthew 6:25

In my own words	SPECKS	I will
	Sin	
	Promise (implied or stated)	
	Example	
	Command (implied or stated)	
	Knowledge	
	Spirit	

44 Spiritual Growth-Bearing Much Fruit

Special Insight

What is your number one priority in life? If God came to you tonight and said that you could ask Him for any one thing you wanted, what would you ask Him for? Would you ask for a longer life? A happier life? Eternal life? More money? A Healthier life? A better marriage? Really, think about it. What one thing would you ask Him for? One night, God actually did appear to Solomon and asked him that very question. God said to the new 12 year-old king, "Ask! What shall I give you?" After Solomon thanked God for the great mercy He had shown to his father David, and telling God, "I am a little child," Solomon humbly asked for wisdom and an understanding heart so that he could rightly judge God's chosen people of Israel. (I Kings 3:9; II Chronicles 1:10). God gave Solomon his request, and granted Solomon more wisdom, understanding, wealth and greater glory than any king who had ever lived before him or anyone who has ever lived since. And yet, Solomon grew arrogant in his knowledge and wealth and became disobedient and dishonoring to God, and found himself "spiritually bankrupt," and without God during most of his adulthood. We see his emptiness expressed throughout his book of Ecclesiastes. So as wonderful as his answer was, it wasn't the best answer anyone could give to the question, "What do you want?" So once again, if you could ask God for anything, what would it be?

Jesus reminds us in His great intercessory prayer in the seventeenth chapter of John, "And this is eternal life, that they might know You, the only true God, and Jesus Christ whom You have sent." (John 17:3). My dear friend. There is truly NOTHING you could ever ask for in this life that is more important or more valuable than the incredible gift of getting to know the Father and Son more intimately. *That* is the ultimate! A man or woman who knows the Father and the Son intimately, even if they were homeless beggars, would be richer than all of earth's billionaires combined. And if you don't understand this; if it does not reflect your heart in a powerful way, then you simply do not understand who Jesus and the Father really are and what an intimate relationship with them can be! Jesus said, "Again, the kingdom of heaven is like treasure hidden in a field, which a man found and hid; and for joy over it he goes and sells all that he has and buys that field." Can you imagine finding a treasure so great even the thought of it consumed you—consumed you to the point you would sell everything you own—everything you ever will own, just to acquire it! That is the magnitude of the incomparable treasure of getting to intimately know the Father and the Son. And that is what the Father offers all of us through the gift of His dear Son. And the more you get to know Jesus, the more you will get to know the Father. And the more you get to know the Father and the Son, the more you will value all that God values. Jesus is the vine and His followers are the branches. Without Him, we can do nothing of eternal significance. But, as we abide in Him, and His words abide in us, we will bear much fruit—and that fruit will be of eternal worth and will bring great glory to the Father.

Additional References for Study: Jesus Speaks, *February 7; Greatest Words,* Fruitbearing *(257-60);*
Chosen (200-02)

Statement of Christ

"Again, the kingdom of heaven is like treasure hidden in a field, which a man found and hid; and for joy over it he goes and sells all that he has and buys that field." Matthew 13:44

In my own words	SPECKS	I will
	Sin	
	Promise (implied or stated)	
	Example	
	Command (implied or stated)	
	Knowledge	
	Spirit	

45 Walk the Narrow Road

Special Insight

Imagine for a moment a new strain of the Bird Flu was now being transmitted through the air, had reached Europe and would soon kill four out of every five people on that continent. Now imagine a new breakout had just begun in New York City. Health officials announce it would soon spread across America with the same devastation it was causing in Europe. But before you panic, they announce a scientist in Colorado has produced a vaccine which is 100% effective, and there's enough for everyone. However, the vaccine cannot be transported. The only way to get it is to travel to the scientist's facility in Royal Gorge, Colorado. The only way to get there is to take Colorado Road 3A, and then cross the narrow Royal Gorge Bridge; a wooden suspension bridge 1,000 feet above the valley below.

Knowing the only vaccine is located across the Royal Gorge, how terrible would it be to deceive people and tell them they could find this life-saving vaccine at their nearest pharmacy? Everyone would rush to their neighborhood pharmacy and only a *few* would make the demanding journey to Royal Gorge. Meanwhile, the local pharmacists are so nice, they give everyone who comes to their store a small paper cup of Kool-Aide, telling them it's just as good as the vaccine in Colorado. Everyone takes it, thinking they're safe. Sadly, a few weeks later, everyone in their family starts to die. How terrible that they believed a lie and relied on a convenient, but fake vaccine. With their lives at stake, they had believed the wrong people. They took the easy path everyone else was taking—the one that only required a brief drive to their nearest pharmacy. Today, people listen to countless voices, proclaiming that all paths lead to God. Even some evangelicals proclaim a message of, "Pray the sinner's prayer and get your free ticket to heaven." Sadly, this is *not* a message Jesus *ever* proclaimed. Jesus said, "Enter through the narrow gate. For wide is the gate and broad is the road that leads to destruction, and many enter through it. But small is the gate and narrow is the road that leads to life, and only a few find it." For centuries, people have said, "That's not fair, how can a God of love be so narrow minded? There should be many ways." The fact is, Jesus can't lie. To say there are many ways, or that it really doesn't matter how a person lives their life, would be a deadly lie that would lead everyone who believed it to an eternity separated from God.

The truth is, God loves us so much that He *did* make a way for anyone to be saved. They don't even have to drive to Royal Gorge to find it. He sent His one and only Son to make the way by sacrificing His life at Calvary. But He not only made the way for anyone to be saved, He told the *truth* about *how* anyone could be saved. He tells all who want to be saved to repent, believe in Him. And when a person truly believes in Christ in their heart, that belief will be expressed by a lifetime of following Him by hearing what He said and doing it. It's not complicated. It's so simple, even a child can repent, believe and follow.

Additional References for Study: Jesus Speaks, *May 22;* Greatest Words, *Narrow Way (170-71);*
Eternal Life (134-42)

Statement of Christ

"But small is the gate and narrow is the road that leads to life, and only a few find it."
Matthew 7:14

In my own words	SPECKS	I will
	Sin	
	Promise (implied or stated)	
	Example	
	Command (implied or stated)	
	Knowledge	
	Spirit	

46 Honor the Son as You Honor the Father

Special Insight

Have you ever been in a courtroom? It's a little scary, even when you've done nothing wrong. When the judge walks in, everyone stands to honor him.   And within a matter of minutes, it's obvious he is in total control. In the courtroom, he is king—he alone holds all authority. He can fine an attorney on either side for contempt. He can dismiss a jury member. He can give a very stern warning to both a defendant and a plaintiff. And if the jury convicts the defendant, the judge determines and pronounces the sentence.   Anyone sitting in the courtroom knows they better honor the judge!   Jesus tells us, "For just as the Father raises the dead and gives them life, even so the Son gives life to whom he is pleased to give it. Moreover, the Father judges no one, but has entrusted all judgment to the Son, that all may honor the Son just as they honor the Father. Whoever does not honor the Son does not honor the Father, who sent him." John 5:21-23

Jesus has the incredible authority and power to give physical life, spiritual life and eternal life! YOU are alive physically, spiritually and eternally because of Jesus! And as if His life-giving power is not enough reason to love and honor Him, in the passage above, Jesus goes on to reveal that the Almighty Father has entrusted all the judgment of mankind to Him.   And if we ascribe and express honor to an earthly judge who only rules only in temporary matters, how much more should we ascribe and express honor to the One whose judgments are eternal?

These revelations are not given to us just to expand our knowledge, but they are given so we may honor the Lord Jesus Christ with all of our being—our heart, mind and soul—so that we will honor Him in our attitudes and our moment-by-moment behavior. They are given so we will also give the highest level of attention and honor to His words.   He has implied in John 12:47-48, when we choose to ignore, minimize or disobey His words, we are rejecting Him. And yet, our Great Shepard doesn't slam us like an earthly judge would if we rejected his words. Jesus tenderly and patiently calls out to us, and leaves "the 99" to safely bring us back into the fold. Oh what a Savior! Hearing His teachings and obeying them is the greatest honor we can express to Him and the Father! That's why He said, "You are My friends if you do whatever I command you." (John 15:14 (NKJV)

Additional References for Study: Jesus Speaks, *July 31;* Greatest Words, *Honoring & Exalting Christ (455-56); Gods Desire (90-92); Reverence for God (110-11)*

Statement of Christ

"That all may honor the Son just as they honor the Father." John 5:23

In my own words	SPECKS	I will
	Sin	
	Promise (implied or stated)	
	Example	
	Command (implied or stated)	
	Knowledge	
	Spirit	

47 Bear Much Fruit

Special Insight

God does not save us, *just* to save us. He saved you and me to be a part of His eternal purpose that is beyond anything we can imagine. Jesus referred to this as bearing fruit—fruit that brings pleasure and glory to the Father. Jesus said, "You did not choose me, but I chose you and appointed you so that you might go and bear fruit —fruit that will last." (John 15:16)

The fruit Jesus is talking about is a life of faith and obedience to His teachings—a life that glorifies God with attitudes, words and deeds flowing naturally out of a heart being transformed by the Holy Spirit.   Fortunately, Jesus tells us how we are going to bear fruit. He said: "I am the vine, you are the branches; **he who abides in Me and I in him**, *he bears* much fruit, for apart from Me you can do nothing." (John 15:5 NASB, emphasis added). A branch doesn't struggle to bear fruit. It simply remains attached to the vine. The vine produces the life-giving sap to flow through the branch to produce its fruit. We don't work to produce the fruit! We simply abide in Christ, and let Christ abide in us. Then, the Holy Spirit flows from Him to us and through us, and produces the fruit, transforming our hearts and everything that flows out of our hearts. We abide in Christ by hearing His words and He abides in us as we act in faith and obey His words. So when we are not bearing fruit, we know we are not spending time in Jesus' words and therefore we may not be acting on them.

Eternal fruit flows out of a heart continually transformed by the washing and regenerating power of Jesus' words.   This happens as you spend time prayerfully meditating on Jesus' teachings. When you do this, you will discover His promises and His commands. As you step out on faith, believing His promises and obeying His commands, you will be *abiding* in Him and He will be abiding in you—and you will bear much fruit in your life and the lives of the people God brings into your path.   The Holy Spirit will produce in you His fruit of love, joy, peace, patience, kindness, goodness, faithfulness, gentleness, and self-control.   Your light will shine, and others will see Christ in you! He will be lifted up in your life, and He will draw others to Himself through you!

Additional References for Study: Jesus Speaks, *August 29, January 5;* Greatest Words, *Fruitbearing (257-60); Following Christ (245-53)*

Statement of Christ

"This is to my Father's glory, that you bear much fruit, showing yourselves to be my disciples."
John 15:8

In my own words	SPECKS	I will
	Sin	
	Promise (implied or stated)	
	Example	
	Command (implied or stated)	
	Knowledge	
	Spirit	

48 Be Full of Light, not Darkness

Special Insight

Solomon said, "Every man's way is right in his own eyes, But the LORD weighs the hearts." (Proverbs 21:2 NASB). Even as sinners saved by grace, our human nature is so dominant, we can rationalize just about anything. We make our behavior the standard by which we wrongfully measure ourselves and others. But God pays no attention to our faulty measurement standards. He weighs our hearts according to *His* standards! No wonder we desperately need His grace and mercy! No wonder we desperately need the atoning work of Christ, and the continuing washing of our hearts and minds! Knowing this to be true, how can we possibly be filled with light? Jesus gives us His wonderful answers in John 8:12, John 15:3-4 and John 8:31-32.

In John 8:12, Jesus said, "I am the Light of the world; he who follows Me will not walk in the darkness, but will have the Light of life." People who do not follow Christ, live in darkness and believe the lies and embrace the values of the *prince* of darkness. And unless they come to Christ, they will remain trapped in darkness and die under the full weight and consequences of their sin.   But here, Jesus announces the glorious, incomprehensible news, that His followers do not have to remain trapped in darkness. They, unlike unbelievers, can walk in His glorious light, and avoid the painful stumbles and deadly falls lying in wait for those who walk in darkness. His followers don't have to lead their lives in spiritual or moral darkness. He is the ultimate light. His life and words are brighter than the brightest star. When we follow Him by imitating His life and letting His words shape our attitudes, and behavior, we will be walking in His continuous light!   The only way to fill our entire heart and mind with light, is to walk in His light. Realize that He said this right after He had saved the woman caught in adultery from being stoned to death. He told her He didn't condemn her and she should leave her path of walking in the darkness of sin.   How could she do it? His immediate answer was for her and anyone else, was to follow Him and walk in His light.

In John 15:3-4, Jesus said, "You are already clean because of the word which I have spoken to you. Abide in Me, and I in you. As the branch cannot bear fruit of itself unless it abides in the vine, so neither can you unless you abide in Me." Jesus' words are not only the light driving the darkness out of our heart, they are the detergents that *cleanse* our heart. As we abide in Him by hearing and doing what He says, His words will continually cleanse the dirt from our hearts that is deposited when we step out of the light and into the darkness. As we have already seen, in John 8:31-32, Jesus tells brand new believers and us that if we will abide (continually live within) His word, we will be His true disciples, we will intimately know the truth, and the truth (referring to Him and the truths revealed by His life and words) will set us free from the terrible taskmaster of sin. Though we will not become sinless, we will have the freedom and power to break away from the paths of darkness and sin and follow Him on His path and in His light. Oh what a Savior! There is none like Him!

Additional References for Study: Jesus Speaks, *January 26;*
Greatest Words, *I am seeing with Spiritual Eyes (230-31)*

Statement of Christ

"Make sure that the light you think you have is not actually darkness. If you are filled with light, with no dark corners, then your whole life will be radiant, as though a floodlight were filling you with light." Luke 11:35-36 (NLT)

In my own words	SPECKS	I will
	Sin	
	Promise (implied or stated)	
	Example	
	Command (implied or stated)	
	Knowledge	
	Spirit	

49 Be like Him – Humble and Gentle in Heart

Special Insight

There's only two ways to follow Jesus—obey His stated teachings and commands, and imitate His life. So when He reveals something about His heart, spirit, attitudes, motivation or purposes, we can assume such revelations *imply* His will in these areas as well. So we treat these implications with the same commitment to follow as we would a stated command. In Matthew 11:29, Jesus reveals He is humble and gentle of heart. Therefore, we can treat this revelation of Him as a revelation of His will for us; and therefore, treat it as an implied command. When He tells us those who are humble will be exalted, He's revealing the reward for those who will obey His teaching to exercise humility. When He tells us that those who are gentle will be blessed and will inherit the earth, He is implying that we should follow Him and be gentle like Him. In Matthew 10:16, He actually gives us a stated command to be as harmless or gentle as doves. He said, "Therefore be wise as serpents and harmless as doves," (NKJV)

Knowing He wants us to be humble and gentle like Him, the question is, "how?"—How can we gain a heart that produces His kind of gentleness and humility? In His life we see His gentleness and humility on display throughout the Gospels. His behavior becomes our example to follow. And Jesus' words provide His instructions on how to behave in a humble and gentle manor. For example, He tells us to focus on the "beam" in our own eye instead of judging another person by focusing on the "speck" in theirs. He tells us to lead our families and others by *serving* them rather than expecting them to serve us! There are dozens of his teachings that tell us how to exercise humility rather than pride or arrogance. And of course His life gives us countless examples, starting with His leaving His glory in heaven to become a baby in a manger, and going to the cross to save us from the eternal consequences of our sin.

The Apostle Peter provides the motivation we should keep in mind every day, when he wrote, "Clothe yourselves with humility toward one another, for GOD IS OPPOSED TO THE PROUD, BUT GIVES GRACE TO THE HUMBLE." (I Peter 5:5 NASB). Do you want to be a constant recipient of God's grace or do you want His opposition? Paul gives us this wonderful reminder in I Corinthians 4:7, when he wrote: "What do you have that you did not receive? And if you did receive it, why do you boast as though you did not?" Everything you and I have that we value, we received from God and others. So what do we have to be proud about? Finally, Peter tells us in I Peter 5:6, "Humble yourselves, therefore, under God's mighty hand, that he may lift you up in due time." My dear friend, humility is not an option. You cannot follow Christ and hold on to your pride and arrogance. You cannot be a continual recipient and vessel of God's grace when you hold on to your pride! See Him as He really is through His words and life and see yourself as you truly are… and humility will become easy!

Additional References for Study: Jesus Speaks, *May 14;* Greatest Words, *Humility (271-3)*
Following Christ (245-47); Spiritual Priorities (328-37)

Statement of Christ

"Take my yoke upon you and learn from me, for I am gentle and humble in heart, and you will find rest for your souls." Matthew 11:29

In my own words	SPECKS	I will
	Sin	
	Promise (implied or stated)	
	Example	
	Command (implied or stated)	
	Knowledge	
	Spirit	

50 Do not Look Back

Special Insight

After Jesus had performed many miracles, including the feeding of the 5,000, a number of men decided they too wanted to follow Him. One man said, "I will follow you, Lord; but first let me go back and say goodbye to my family." While that seemed like a perfectly reasonable request, to Jesus, it wasn't reasonable at all! He replied, "No one who puts a hand to the plow and looks back is fit for service in the kingdom of God." You see, that man was wanting to postpone His following of Christ "in the present," in order to take time to go back and focus on that which was part of his *past*. His past life was focused entirely on that which was self-centered and temporal. By following Christ, he would be focusing on the kingdom of God, serving the Master instead of himself, and pursuing that which was eternal. Comparing his temporal, self-centered past and its temporal gratification, with service for the kingdom of God and eternal glory was a foolish choice. A choice that revealed that he truly had no idea who Jesus really was and the eternal importance of what Jesus 4 was doing. So the man traded his opportunity for making an eternal impact and serving Christ, for going back and dwelling in the past.

In this revelation, Jesus gives us two implied commands. First, don't be like this man who sacrificed the glory of the eternal purposes and callings of Christ for the temporal gratifications your past life offers. Second, don't look back when you are following Christ. Don't live in the past. You can't plow a straight furrow in the field when the oxen is moving forward and you are looking backward. Living in the past, whether five minutes ago or five years ago, prevents you from living in and focusing on the *current* moment. When our mind or heart sets our eyes on the past, we cannot serve Christ in the present. When we live in the future we are distracted and tormented by worries, fears and stresses, all of which only appear when we are dwelling in the future. When we turn our eyes to the past, sadness, regret, anger and bitterness appear and enter our mind and heart. BUT, when our mind and heart dwell squarely in the moment we are in, we can experience the true presence of the living Christ. He only dwells in the present moment—never in the past or future. When we force our eyes, minds and hearts to dwell in the moment, we can experience all that He is and all that He has. We can hear and respond to the promptings of the Holy Spirit. We can experience His love and kindness for those who share the moment with us. You cannot be looking back and expect to experience the miracle of His presence in the moment.

Jesus wants you to know He has called you into a life of eternal purpose. Every day, He sets you into fields ripe for harvest! What He told His disciples in John 4:36 is just as true for you and I right now, as it was for His disciples then. He said, "Even now the one who reaps draws a wage and harvests a crop for eternal life, so that the sower and the reaper may be glad together." Any time you find yourself drifting into the past, don't panic, just come back into the moment and follow your Shepherd.

Additional References for Study: Jesus Speaks, *January 7;* Greatest Words, *Lining in the Present (277-78)*

Statement of Christ

"No one who puts a hand to the plow and looks back is fit for service in the kingdom of God."
Luke 9:62

In my own words	SPECKS	I will
	Sin	
	Promise (implied or stated)	
	Example	
	Command (implied or stated)	
	Knowledge	
	Spirit	

51 Be on Guard for All Kinds of Greed

Special Insight

Have you ever been robbed by a thief? Twice I have been robbed. One time thieves broke into a car that I had rented in Hawaii and stole my only camera and a wrist watch. Another time, a drug addict broke into our house when my wife and children were at home and stole some cash and things from our bedroom. When you are robbed, you really feel terribly violated.

Solomon tells us that greed is a merciless thief that steals the very *life* of the one who possesses it. Terribly, the life that greed steals isn't merely one's temporary life on earth—it can steal a person's soul and replace God as the Lord and Master of a person's life. It is why Jesus warned, "Watch out! Be on your guard against all kinds of greed." Equally scary, He said, "No one can serve two masters. Either he will hate the one and love the other, or he will be devoted to one and despise the other. You cannot serve both God and Money." (Matthew 6:24). When greed steals the ruling throne of your life, you become a lover of that which you are greedy for, and in God's eyes, you become a *hater* of God!

You may be like me and initially reply, "Thank heavens I'm not greedy." (Oh no, that sounds like the Pharisee who looked at the sinner and said, 'Thank God I'm not like him.") The truth is, all of us struggle with greed. It's built into our human nature. Most of us never think of ourselves as greedy because we compare ourselves to people we know or have heard about who are driven or consumed by greed. But God doesn't compare us to others or our hearts to the hearts of others. Instead, He compares us to His nature and the standards of His word. We can be greedy for money or material possessions; we can even be greedy for another person (their time, attention or affection). Greed simply means longing for *more* of something than we can righteously acquire.

Jesus also compares greed to weeds that choke the life out of that which creates a love for God and a desire to intimately know and follow Christ. But weeds never start their life as weeds; they start as *seeds* that ultimately grow into weeds. Jesus tells us to watch out and be on guard against every kind of greed so we won't have our spiritual life choked out of us.

There are two ways to deal with the weeds of greed. The best way is to daily kill the seeds before they sprout, by *abiding* in Jesus' words daily. This continually makes us His true disciples, continually reveals the truth about God's desires and our desires, and sets us free from our enslavement to our sin nature. (John 8:31-32). The second way to deal with the weeds of greed is to pull out the sprouts as soon as we notice them. We do this whenever we become aware of a seed of greed through reading the Word of God or through the prompting of the Holy Spirit. Every day look at Jesus' life and words to discern those things that have eternal worth, and pursue them. Every day focus your thoughts on the wondrous blessings your Heavenly Father has given you. This will produce a heart of continual gratefulness.

Additional References for Study: Jesus Speaks, *February 4;* Greatest Words, *Wealth & Possession (344-47)*

Statement of Christ

"Watch out! Be on your guard against all kinds of greed; life does not consist in an abundance of possessions." Luke 12:15

In my own words	SPECKS	I will
	Sin	
	Promise (implied or stated)	
	Example	
	Command (implied or stated)	
	Knowledge	
	Spirit	

52 Rejoice and Be Glad When You Suffer for Righteousness Sake

Special Insight

A dear friend of mine had a sweet, amazing teenage son—a boy who was like bottled sunshine. He was thoughtful, helpful, considerate, caring and kind. He was also short. When his family moved into a new school district, he became the victim of a great deal of bullying and ridicule. It seems the "big guys" at his new high school had a problem with a guy that was always radiantly happy. This sweet fifteen year-old Christian finally couldn't take it any more. And in a moment of despair and desperation, killed himself. This wonderful young man had enjoyed a lifetime of religion and religious activity. But I don't think anyone ever helped him to understand that when you suffer for righteousness sake, it's not a tragedy —it's a means of experiencing the suffering and persecution that Jesus and God's glorious prophets experienced. He didn't know that his bullies, though they were subjecting him to fear and humiliation, were unknowingly storing up treasures in heaven for him. Jesus said that suffering for righteousness sake is a great blessing. He said, "Blessed are those who are persecuted because of righteousness, for theirs is the kingdom of heaven. Blessed are you when people insult you, persecute you and falsely say all kinds of evil against you because of me. Rejoice and be glad, because great is your reward in heaven, for in the same way they persecuted the prophets who were before you." (Matthew 5:12-12)

Children must learn this truth. When they suffer for righteousness sake, they are experiencing what the Apostle Paul called, "the fellowship of His (Christ's) suffering," and treasures in heaven are being stored up for them. (Philippians 3:10). He told the believers in Corinth who were undergoing tremendous persecution, "For momentary, light affliction is producing for us an eternal weight of glory far beyond all comparison, while we look not at the things which are seen, but at the things which are not seen; for the things which are seen are temporal, but the things which are not seen are eternal." (II Corinthians 4:17-18). Dear friend, Jesus' command to "rejoice and be glad," when you suffer for righteousness sake, is not just for kids—it's for you and me as well. Today, Christians are being ridiculed, lied about, viciously attacked verbally and physically, and even martyred. Those who promote and participate in such evil behavior think they are hurting us. In reality, they are bringing us eternal glory beyond all comparison, and storing up for themselves an eternal life filled with the wrath of the Almighty God.

But Jesus doesn't just tell us to rejoice and be glad when such evils are committed against us. He tells us, "Love your enemies, do good to those who hate you, bless those who curse you, pray for those who mistreat you." Pray that they will be redeemed, as Saul, the great hater and persecutor of the early church was. Christianity's most vile persecutor, became the Apostle Paul, it's greatest evangelist! I wonder which persecuted believers prayed for that "chief of sinners?" What an amazing testimony of God's mercy and grace our dear brother Saul/Paul became.

Additional References for Study: Jesus Speaks, *January 18;* Greatest Words,
Rejections and Persecution of Christians (308-12)

Statement of Christ

"Rejoice and be glad, because great is your reward in heaven, for in the same way they persecuted the prophets who were before you." Matthew 5:12 (NASB)

In my own words	SPECKS	I will
	Sin	
	Promise (implied or stated)	
	Example	
	Command (implied or stated)	
	Knowledge	
	Spirit	

About Knowing Him

We are a non-denominational ministry dedicated to providing materials and discipleship for all who want to know Christ more intimately.

FOUNDERS

Steven K. Scott

He is the New York Times best-selling author of numerous books, including The Greatest Words Ever Spoken, The Jesus Mission, and The Riches Man Who Ever Lived. Using the laws of success he learned from the book of Proverbs, Scott and his partners have built more than a dozen highly successful US and international companies. In his teaching ministry, Scott emphasizes the unique role and miraculous power of Jesus' words in the lives of believers. He says, "As we abide in Jesus' words, we can experience His fullness and come to know Him more intimately than we have ever imagined."

Michael Smalley, Ph.D.

Michael specializes in teaching people the principles of how to live out Jesus' greatest commands to love God and love others. His popularity as a renowned marriage and relationship expert quickly grew through his humorous stories and straightforward, no-nonsense advice. Michael's message inspires, motivates and challenges people to build better relationships.

His love story with his wife Amy began while he was an undergraduate at Baylor University. After graduation, Michael went on to earn a master's degree in clinical psychology from Wheaton College outside Chicago, Illinois and finished his Ph.D. at Barnham Theological Seminar in Houston, Texas.

Michael is the President of Knowing Him and also a co-founder, along with his wife Amy, of Smalley Institute and its premiere program for couples in crisis, the Reignite Marriage Intensive program. Traditional marriage counseling can be lengthy and frustrating and often couples can't find the time to make a positive impact on their relationships. Currently, the Smalley Institute has eight locations across the United States and even one in South Africa!

He has enjoyed over 22 years of marriage and makes his home in Magnolia, Texas. Michael has three children, Cole, Reagan, and David.